SEPARATES
THAT
TRAVEL

THE TIME-LIFE LIBRARY OF BOATING
HUMAN BEHAVIOR
THE ART OF SEWING
THE OLD WEST
THE EMERGENCE OF MAN
THE AMERICAN WILDERNESS
THE TIME-LIFE ENCYCLOPEDIA OF GARDENING
LIFE LIBRARY OF PHOTOGRAPHY
THIS FABULOUS CENTURY
FOODS OF THE WORLD
TIME-LIFE LIBRARY OF AMERICA
TIME-LIFE LIBRARY OF ART
GREAT AGES OF MAN
LIFE SCIENCE LIBRARY
THE LIFE HISTORY OF THE UNITED STATES
TIME READING PROGRAM
LIFE NATURE LIBRARY
LIFE WORLD LIBRARY
FAMILY LIBRARY:
    HOW THINGS WORK IN YOUR HOME
    THE TIME-LIFE BOOK OF THE FAMILY CAR
    THE TIME-LIFE FAMILY LEGAL GUIDE
    THE TIME-LIFE BOOK OF FAMILY FINANCE

THE ART OF SEWING

SEPARATES THAT TRAVEL

BY THE EDITORS OF TIME-LIFE BOOKS

TIME-LIFE BOOKS, NEW YORK

THE ART OF SEWING
EDITORIAL STAFF FOR
SEPARATES THAT TRAVEL
EDITOR: Fred R. Smith
Designer: Virginia Gianakos
Assistant Designer: Elaine Zeitsoff
Text Editors: Betsy Frankel, Anne Horan,
Gerry Schremp
Picture Editor: Kathy Ritchell
Chief Researcher: Wendy A. Rieder
Staff Writers: Sondra R. Albert, Don Earnest,
Marian Gordon Goldman, Angela D. Goodman,
Susan Hillaby, Marilyn Kendig, Jill Spiller,
Sandra Streepey, Reiko Uyeshima
Research Staff: Laura James, Cinda Siler,
Ginger Seippel, Lyn Stallworth, Diane Asselin,
Doris Coffin
Art Staff: Anne B. Landry (art manager),
Angela Alleyne, Penny Burnham,
Patricia Byrne, Catherine Caufield,
Jean Held
Editorial Assistant: Anne Gordon

EDITORIAL PRODUCTION
Production Editor: Douglas B. Graham
Assistant Production Editors:
Gennaro C. Esposito, Feliciano Madrid
Quality Director: Robert L. Young
Assistant Quality Director: James J. Cox
Associate: Serafino J. Cambareri
Copy Staff: Eleanore W. Karsten (chief),
Kathleen Beakley, Ricki Tarlow, Florence Keith,
Pearl Sverdlin
Picture Department: Dolores A. Littles,
Susan Hearn
Traffic: Carmen McLellan

THE CONSULTANTS
Gretel Courtney taught for several years at the
French Fashion Academy in New York City. She
has studied patternmaking and design at the
Fashion Institute of Technology in New York and
haute couture at the French Fashion Academy.

Tracy Kendall has for many years designed sets
and costumes for commercial films and advertis-
ing. She is currently a fashion stylist.

Julian Tomchin is a textile designer who has re-
ceived the Vogue Fabric Award and a Coty
Award of the American Fashion Critics. A grad-
uate of Syracuse University's Fine Arts College,
he has been chairman of the Textile Design Department at the Shenkar College of Fashion and
Textile Technology in Tel Aviv and now teaches
at the Parsons School of Design in New York.

Valuable assistance was provided by these
departments and individuals of Time Inc.:
Editorial Production, Norman Airey; Library,
Benjamin Lightman; Picture Collection, Doris
O'Neil; Photographic Laboratory, George Karas;
TIME-LIFE News Service, Murray J. Gart;
Correspondents Margot Hapgood and Dorothy
Bacon (London), Ann Natanson (Rome),
Josephine du Brusle (Paris).

CONTENTS

1
CLOTHES TO TAKE FOR A TRIP

Around the turn of the century, every self-respecting traveler had a trunk—a hide-covered, brass-bound box that was big enough to hold all the owner's clothing, and a spare Bible as well. "Whenever you went anywhere, you took a trunk," wrote one Maine Yankee, reminiscing about village life, "and whenever you coursed a 'depot' platform you had to dodge expressmen pulling on their hand wagons of trunks."

LIGHTWEIGHT AND CAREFREE ON THE GO

No more. What trunks survive today are generally gathering dust in the attic—perhaps storing long-unused costumes like the duster *(overleaf)* that ladies wore touring in the then-new motor car. In the age of the jet, every air traveler is mindful of weight limitations. Even those who travel by ship, train or car tend to travel light. With careful planning, anyone can pack a small but versatile wardrobe into a single suitcase—and be imaginatively dressed for all occasions.

The secret to such versatility is making that wardrobe of separates: skirts and pants, shirts, vests, sweaters and jackets that can be worn in interchangeable combinations. How far this idea can be exploited is indicated by television reporter Betty Rollin, whose job makes travel a part of her daily life. She gets an attractive wardrobe into a tote bag: "I take a skirt that doesn't get dirty easily and three tops: a T-shirt or a heavyweight all-wool sweater, depending on the climate I'm going to; a blazer or maybe a cardigan that may or may not be worn with the T-shirt or the sweater, and consequently gives me a different look; and then for evening a special top—something low-cut and dressy, maybe a silk knit—that can go with the same skirt."

Separates that travel well almost always serve well at home but the reverse is not necessarily true. For 20th Century mobility, clothes must meet several requirements:

Light weight, so that a costume is not tiring to wear (or carry).

Temperature adaptability, to keep a flight south from bringing on shivers in Copenhagen and perspiration in Nice.

Elasticity, for comfort during five or six hours strapped into a narrow seat.

Shape retention so clothes will not look as if they have been slept in even when they have been.

Crease resistance and easy care for places where dry cleaners and washing machines may be hard to find.

Minimum structure, for comfort and easy packing in a small space.

Separates generally meet these requirements better than dresses, particularly when made in simple styles that take advantage of recent fabric developments: strong and shape-holding fibers, woven cloth that has been chemically treated to stay fresh-looking longer, and the comfortable, adaptable knits (pages 24-25). Sewing with these fabrics calls for modifications of customary techniques (pages 34-35), for the very characteristics that make the materials so useful for separates may make them hard to cut or slippery in the sewing machine.

For both woven and knitted materials, man-made fibers add special values. "Polyester is *the* travel fabric," insists Anita Pasalbessy, sportswear buyer for Abercrombie & Fitch, the store that specializes in outfitting people for Pago Pago, Zambia and Hudson's Bay. "It never needs pressing, and it dries in a trice."

Those advantages are secondary to Virginia Haynes, whose career as a cosmetics executive keeps her traveling four months out of every 12. She finds counterbalancing virtues in the traditional fibers. "I like natural fabrics better than polyesters—wool for cool climates, cotton for hot ones. Polyesters pull and discolor; natural fabrics last better in the long run. As for creases, the first thing I do when I get to a hotel is unpack and let my clothes hang—in the bathroom steam if need be. If they still have wrinkles that won't hang out, I borrow an iron from the hotel. Not many people know you can do that."

In any fabric, the grandmother of today's travel separates (and to many, still the preeminent style) is the shirtwaist blouse, which in one form or another has survived for more than three quarters of a century, during the waxing and waning of long skirts and miniskirts, full skirts and slim skirts, pants, shorts and culottes—to all of which it has served as foil and companion.

The original appearance of the shirtwaist coincided with the entrance of women into the working world. It was the first piece of women's wear to be mass produced; it was easily manufactured, just as it is easily made at home today. At prices as low as 50 cents per top, the working girl could afford several different shirtwaists, to change the look of the basic skirt that she might wear for several days.

The shirtwaist became a fad overnight, and in less than a decade it had climbed the social ladder. "Its permanency seems assured," predicted a trade journal called *The Cutter-Up.* "It is worn by rich and poor alike, is ornate or simple, and lends itself to fashionable use, no matter what the occasion."

The poor working girl's shirtwaist may still be the starting point for a traveler's mix-and-match wardrobe, but today other styles *(pages 102-103, 156-157)* offer versatility. Almost any simple designs can be combined if coordinated by color and pattern.

Color is the first consideration in putting together a wardrobe of interchangeable parts. Says Catherine Lis, manager of the international shopping service at Saks Fifth Avenue, "The traveler should pick two color schemes—only two—no more than two. I can't stress this enough." These two colors serve as the basics around which she will coordinate everything else. But the basic color need not be dull. "Black, beige, white and gray aren't the only basics," says Judy Krull, head of customer fashion service at Bloomingdale's department store. "I've based some of my favorite outfits on lilac and forest green."

Once the traveler has decided on the color schemes to use, travel author Myra Waldo advises: "Count the number of days you will be in one place and plan for that stay. Then you can repeat and repeat, and your look to new people will always be new." But, she cautions, "Keep everything low-keyed. Prints should be subtle, not staggering ones that will remain in everyone's mind, including your own."

The importance of fabric, color and pattern in travel clothes sometimes obscures an equally essential factor: structure. Elaborately shaped garments may crush easily in the suitcase and almost as easily when worn all day in a car or plane. They may also be uncomfortable, for most shaping is designed to approximate the body when it is standing or sitting politely—not curled in a ball for a mid-flight nap or stretching to clamber around the Coliseum. The relatively unstructured design of many separates —particularly knits—is one of their key advantages to the traveler.

Yet there are some structural details that are little more than stylistic touches at home but temper-saving conveniences afield. To accommodate the whimsies of weather and exotic heating systems, snug-fitting cuffs and jacket waists *(pages 66-70)* are comfortable; so are neckline openings that easily button or zip to whatever level temperature or modesty demands. For relaxation, put stretchable waistbands on skirts and pants; for pure handiness, do not forget pockets.

"For traveling there is nothing like pockets," says Jean Campbell, designer of Sportwhirl Clothes. They can hold candy bars, scarves, extra film—the things the traveler often wants ready or forgets to put into the suitcase until after it is locked shut.

Pockets can be worked into the gathers of full skirts, nestled below the waist or against the hip, where they hardly show; or they can be made a decorative feature that stands out and meets the eye—on the front of a skirt, on the back of a pair of pants —even on sleeves and the sides of pants legs, like carpenters' pockets. For travel practicality they must be positioned properly; a back pocket should not be so low that the wearer will sit on it and crush the con-

tents; arm pockets and leg pockets should be placed either high or low, but not at mid-limb, where they will interfere with the bending of elbow and knee.

Finally, by adding jewelry, which can change the character of the separates (making them elegant or casual); scarves, which can accentuate some colors and play down others; and a minimum of two pairs of shoes —one for walking, another for evening—the travel wardrobe of separates is assembled. All of it, save the shoes and jewelry, can be made by the home seamstress before she sets off. Moreover, all of it will serve just as well in a peripatetic day at home as it does journeying to far-flung places.

Five 1906 ladies model the latest in "dusters," fashion's answer to the hazards of travel in open cars over unpaved roads. Dusters came in various weaves of cotton, silk and linen—usually in white, tan or lemon yellow. The filmy veil, drawn over the face once the lady was carborne, might be of any color, but emerald green was thought to be most effective for guarding feminine complexions against unthinkable suntan.

Separates for all occasions

Half the fun of going on a trip is taking a wardrobe that sails smoothly through every social situation. Coats that go over slacks or long skirts; beach robes that double as dressing gowns; play clothes that leave the beach for lunch in a bistro; street clothes that cope with showers or unseasonable chills; and evening clothes that emerge from a postage-stamp-sized space in the suitcase —all make traveling effortless.

Ideally, this hard-working wardrobe is made up of lightweight, crushproof parts that change like chameleons, depending upon the accessories worn with them—and that wash in a hotel hand-basin and dry on a coat hanger overnight.

Waiting at the airport, three travelers wear *(left to right)* a washable pseudo-suede coat and hat with wool flannel pants and sweater; a lightweight mohair jacket with wool flannel skirt and drip-dry blouse; and a wool-knit wrap coat over a two-piece knitted dress with beret.

These three convertible costumes could go from the beach to lunch on the hotel terrace. At left is a halter-neck nylon jersey dress with a drawstring top; for other occasions the drawstring becomes a gathered waistline and the dress an ankle-length skirt. At center are four pieces easily juggled: a safari jacket and button-front skirt in permanent-press cotton polyester cover a pair of matching shorts and a knitted strapless top. At right, stretch cotton terry-cloth shorts and bare-midriff top serve for sunning and swimming, while the matching beach cover-up could double as a bathrobe.

For sightseeing around town during the day, the choice *(left to right)* includes permanent-press cotton-polyester pants worn with a cotton T-shirt tunic that could also function alone as a dress; a two-piece knitted dress of nonwrinkling wool and rayon whose separate parts can be tops or bottoms for other ensembles; and a permanent-press cotton poplin rain suit with a dual personality—both jacket and skirt reverse to sleek nylon ciré.

Three glamorous possibilities for after-dark dressing take advantage of fabrics that shed wrinkles and require little luggage space. Below, a dramatically striped blouse and skirt of knitted wool have stripes running one way in the top, the other way in the skirt. A polyester crusader's tunic *(center)* with sleeves vented to the elbow is worn with silk pants. A two-piece dress *(right)* of permanently crinkled pleats ends in frills at the bodice and skirt hems.

2
OUT OF THE SUITCASE, READY TO WEAR

E verybody rides in public vehicles in these democratic days," observed Georgiana Hill in 1893, bemoaning a custom that tended to produce a sober uniformity of dress. "Everything for daily use must be quiet and unnoticeable, able to withstand wear and tear, rain and dust, tumbling and creasing. The omnibus and tram car," she concluded crisply, "have a lot to answer for."

Today Georgiana's opinions are no long-

THE PICK OF THE PACKABLE FABRICS

er valid. Thanks to a revolution in fabric technology, it is perfectly possible for travelers to be fashionably dressed en route in as many colors, patterns and textures as they like and to arrive at their destination virtually untumbled and uncreased. Better yet, the clothes they pack in their luggage will emerge ready to wear with little more than a quick shakeout. Some of these well-behaved fabrics are updated versions of classics like seersucker and mummy cloth, whose permanent puckers defy wrinkles because they are already intentionally wrinkled. More often than not, however, these traditional favorites are no longer made of cotton or linen, but of blends of natural and synthetic fibers.

The synthetics in fact are a major part of the fabric revolution. Inherently easy to wash, quick drying and resistant to wrinkling, they have enormously expanded the range of fabrics that travel well. Polyester, acrylic and nylon lend their carefree qualities to blends of cotton, silk and wool, and in addition have acquired so many refinements that they have spawned a whole new breed of synthetic textiles.

Typically extruded in a semiliquid state from a device that looks like a shower head, synthetic filaments can take many forms. They are stretched while still viscous, twisted and textured, and heat-treated to give them a permanent character from which they will never vary. In fact they can be given almost any property desired.

For instance, there are polyester filaments stretched so fine that fabrics made from them rival silk in their fluidity, and one process gives acrylic the luxuriant feel of cashmere. Even the nonabsorbency that once made synthetic fabrics uncomfortable in hot weather has been virtually eliminated. Impregnated with a special chemical that behaves like a wick, synthetics can be almost as breathable as cotton.

Though many of these improved synthetics go into woven cloth, the majority are gobbled up by knitting mills, whose products are of course the best travelers of all. From Coco Chanel's revolutionary introduction of unstructured jersey dresses of the '20s —the first knits to reach the ranks of high fashion—knitted fabrics have come far. Machines are as versatile as computer technology can make them, and so are the fabrics made on them, ranging from openwork filigree to sturdy knitted cloth with the stability of woven fabric.

Chief among these sturdy knits are the ubiquitous double knits, which are actually rib knits made by two sets of needles that interlock to create a double layer of fabric. When made of synthetic yarns, with their even, continuous filaments, and on sophisticated knitting machines, double knits account for a remarkable number of new fabrics. One new version of polyester double knit, for instance, is as light and filmy as georgette or voile; another is ribbed and napped in a replica of corduroy; while a third is embossed in an imitation of grained leather.

Perhaps the most amazing of the new synthetic fabrics are those that imitate suede. They are made in various combinations of nylon, rayon, acrylic, polyester and polyurethane—depending upon the manufacturer's formula. Some pseudo suedes are made by a process that bypasses both knitting and weaving; others come double-faced or single-faced with either a woven or knitted base. Ranging in price from four dollars to $30 a yard, the best of them are almost indistinguishable from the real thing —but unlike real suede, most are washable. In addition, they never need pressing, and garments made from them will arrive at their destination untumbled and uncreased, whatever the conveyance.

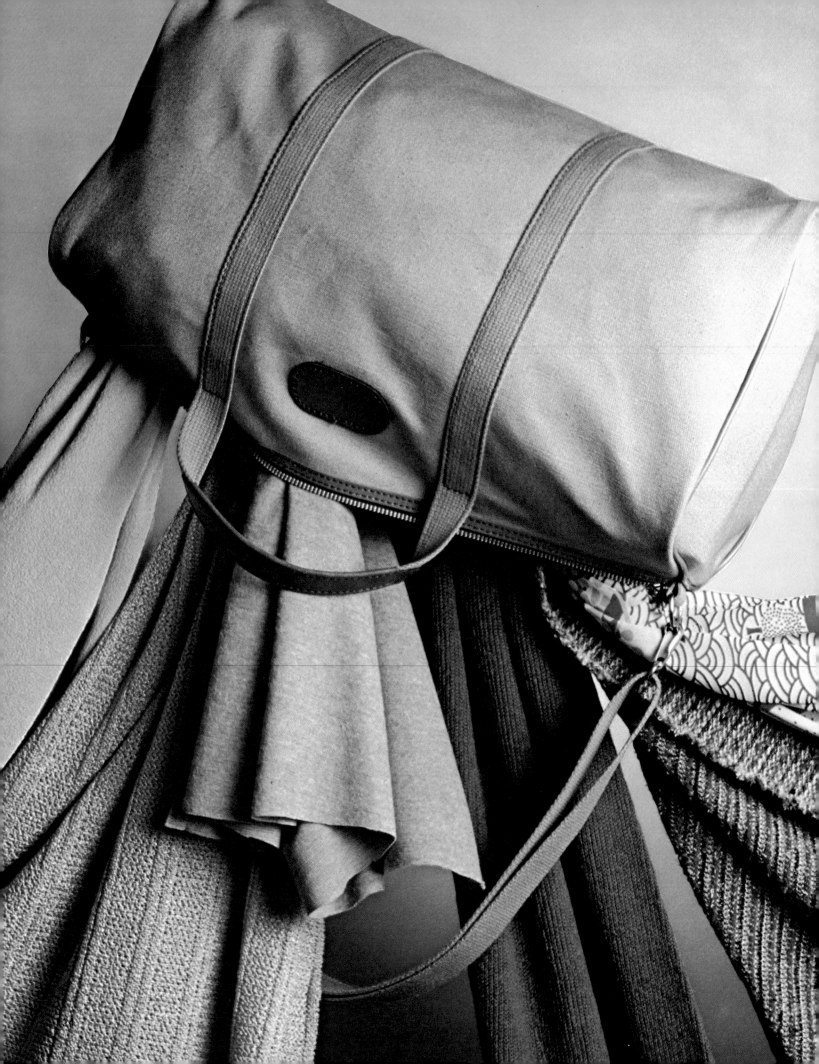

Knits for traveling the world

As more and more people take to the road for pleasure or business, an abundance of new and updated fabrics accommodates their need for light, easy-to-care-for clothes that stay fresh-looking after hours of wear or confinement in a suitcase.

Knits like those cascading out of the duffel bag shown here are a case in point. Particularly comfortable to wear in transit because they never constrict movement, their loose, springy construction also means they bounce back into shape after tight packing.

A sampling of the enormous variety available includes *(left to right)* a casual acrylic-and-polyester stretch terry, a shimmery nylon in a lacy stripe, a double-knit of polyester and acrylic softened with rabbit hair, a purple sweater knit of pure wool, a novelty knit called "mish-mash" by its manufacturer, who created it with all his leftover yarn, and a nylon-and-triacetate jersey printed with an Art Deco design.

Cloth wrinkled on purpose

One way to solve the problem of rumpled clothes is to choose fabrics with wrinkles built in, like all the fabrics here. The cotton-polyester blend at right and flowered cotton plissé beside it have been treated chemically to pucker; the next fabric, a classic Indian cotton, and its checked version, at the very bottom, acquire their texture from naturally creped yarns. Between them are a crushed velvet whose streaky surface is applied with heated rollers, and a cotton plaid seersucker whose ripples are made by alternating the thread tension during weaving.

Fibers that fight wrinkles

Many man-made fabrics are by their very nature wrinkle shedding because the fibers of which they are made are more resilient than natural fibers. An added advantage for the traveler is that they are all washable.

The delicate chevron-patterned polyester pongee at top looks and feels like fine cotton, while next to it nonwoven pseudo suede is an almost perfect (and washable) imitation of the real thing. Creases in the sturdy cotton-polyester duck *(center right)* will fall out after it is hung for a few hours, while both the geometrically patterned nylon satin and the rayon-polyester voile print can be worn immediately after unpacking.

Finally, at the extreme left, a wool tweed mixed with polyester and nylon is not only crease-resistant but can actually be laundered.

A guide to working with knitted fabrics

The stretchiness that makes knits unsurpassed for travel clothes also introduces special problems in sewing with them. Each type has individual properties that affect how it should be handled. These characteristics depend primarily on stretchiness, which varies from very elastic to quite firm, depending upon the resilience of the yarn used, the size of the stitch and the particular pattern of stitches that are produced by the knitting machine. In rib knits, for instance, the combination of knitting and purling introduces a great deal of stretch, while in double knits the interlocking action of two sets of needles creates a fabric with almost as much stability as woven cloth. Knits can also vary in thickness from featherweight jerseys to bulky sweater-knits, and these differences too call for the use of special sewing techniques.

When shopping for knitted fabrics, be sure to examine them for visible flaws; knits tend to snag easily and a snag can quickly lead to a run. Check to see that the rows of crosswise loops or ribs lie at right angles to those that run lengthwise, then pull the fabric in both directions to determine if it recovers its original shape when you let it go. Finally, try to crush the fabric, to be sure that the wrinkles you make spring out when released.

GENERAL DESCRIPTION

RELATIVELY STABLE KNITS

These fabrics closely resemble woven fabrics in feel. Lengthwise stretch is negligible; crosswise stretch is about 15 to 20 per cent. Most double knits fall into this category.

MODERATELY STRETCHY KNITS

Somewhat less firm than relatively stable knits, these fabrics cling slightly. The crosswise stretch is about 20 to 30 per cent; the lengthwise stretch is the same or slightly less.

VERY STRETCHY KNITS

These fabrics behave like hand knits; they stretch in both directions, usually between 40 to 60 per cent, though sometimes a great deal more. They cling very closely to the body. They should always be stored flat (they may stretch out of shape on hangers).

LIGHTWEIGHT KNITS

Thin, supple and sometimes diaphanous, these fabrics are not only stretchy but also drape and cling to the body, and have practically no bulk.

BULKY KNITS

Whether fluffy or flat, stretchy or moderately stretchy, these fabrics have a thick, resilient feel and are often loosely constructed.

PATTERN SELECTION	FABRIC HANDLING	ACCESSORIES	SEWING TIPS
Because knits fit more closely than woven fabrics, patterns for them require less ease; the amount of ease needed depends on the stretchiness of the knit. To gauge whether a knit is relatively stable, moderately stretchy or very stretchy, see page 34. To judge a pattern's suitability for each knit type, see below. The ease needed at the bustline is generally 1 or 2 inches (as much as 3 inches for firm knits and loose-fitting styles); for a sleeve, 1 inch; for the sleeve cap, 3/4 to 1 inch; for the hip, 1 to 2 inches.	Preshrink fabric by washing or dry cleaning, as specified on the label. Preshrink notions that are not polyester or nylon, except ribbing trims. Nonwoven interfacing needs no preshrinking, but woven interfacing does; the fusible kind should be dried flat, fusible side up. Use a pattern layout for napped fabrics, since knits are directional. Pull the edges of a knitted fabric; if it runs, place the pattern pieces so the runs are hidden in the hem. If the edges curl in cutting, flatten with spray starch.	Use ballpoint needles in the finest size suitable for the fabric weight and density. In fine needles (Sizes 9-11), use Size A silk or nylon thread, or fine polyester; in medium needles (Size 14), regular polyester or cotton-polyester thread. Sharp scissors are essential; dull scissors will drag flexible knits out of alignment. For very slithery knits, use scissors with a serrated lower blade. Other aids that simplify working with knits are special presser feet (pages 44-45) and ballpoint or fine steel pins.	Since knitted fabrics use more yarn per inch than woven fabrics, lint builds up faster; machines must be cleaned often. Synthetic knits and threads leave residues on needles, blunting or roughening them; change needles often and use an emery or conditioning pad (page 45). If seams pucker or the machine skips: clean the machine; clean or change the needle; shorten the stitch; try a finer needle and thread; loosen tension. To keep shoulder seams from stretching, stabilize with tape (page 79).
Use patterns suitable for woven fabrics of similar weight, but fit the garment closer to the body. Use standard zipper or button openings, however, for these fabrics will not stretch enough to slip over hips or head. Pattern styles shaped by darts as well as by eased seams are suitable.	Use an L-shaped square (page 34) to establish a straight crosswise edge. Stay stitch (Glossary) necklines and waistlines with a straight stitch, setting the machine at 10 to 12 stitches to the inch.	Shrinkproof or preshrunk standard zippers, underlinings and interfacings can be used with firm knitted fabrics; knits conform to dimensions of the materials used with them. Attach fusible interfacings to facings or surfaces that do not show on the finished garment. Mark with dressmaker's carbon and a smooth-edged tracing wheel.	Sew with basic stretch seams (page 78). On double knits which do not curl, seam allowances can be left unfinished and trimmed to 3/8 inch to lessen bulk.
Patterns suggested for knits are recommended. If standard patterns are used, choose simple styles with a minimum of darts and fitting and purchase patterns a size smaller than usual; eliminate any excess ease when the garment is fitted on the body. These fabrics are sufficiently stretchy for pullover necklines and pull-on waistlines.	Lay out preshrunk fabric and establish both lengthwise and crosswise straight edges with an L-shaped square, following the method described on page 34.	Zippers with knitted tapes are recommended; elastic waistbands can be substituted for waistline zippers. Use interfacings designed especially for knits, and then only in such areas as necklines, collars and cuffs; underlinings are not recommended. An overedge presser foot eliminates curling and bunching in narrow seams.	Make seams by either stretch seam method (page 78). Use tape to prevent stretching in seams bearing weight (shoulders, waistlines and armholes). When finishing hems by hand, use two rows of catch-stitching (Appendix), one in the middle of the hem and the other just below the top edge. Eliminate facings where possible; use bound edges.
Look for patterns designed especially for stretchy knits. Otherwise, choose a pattern labeled "suitable for knits," one size smaller. Pull-on and similar sweater styles are especially suitable.	Allow preshrunk fabric to lie flat for several hours or overnight, to "relax" to its natural shape. Mark lengthwise and crosswise straight edges with an L-shaped square (page 34). To keep fabric from stretching during cutting, do not let any part of it hang over the cutting surface edge. If the fabric slips in cutting, pin to a backing of tissue paper.	Underlinings and interfacings are not recommended. Zippers, if used, should have knitted tapes. Use an overedge presser foot to keep narrow seam allowances from curling. In straight or fine zigzag stitching, use a special small-hole throat plate to keep the fabric from poking through the hole, or use tissue paper under the fabric.	Make seams by either of the stretch methods (page 78) or the hand-felled method (page 79). Use tape to prevent stretching in seams that bear weight. Finish hems by hand using two rows of catch-stitching (Appendix), one in the middle of the hem and the other just below the top edge, or use rib-knit edging, as described on pages 71-72.
Choose styles that are either clinging and close-fitting, or are soft, with draped effects or flowing gathers. Avoid styles that are rigidly structured.	Handle delicate knits with care, to avoid snagging; if laundering to preshrink them, place them in a mesh bag. To cut a slippery fabric, pin it to tissue paper to hold it in place, or lay it on a soft surface such as toweling or carpet so that the scissor blade will not stretch it out of shape.	Use a Size 9 or 11 ballpoint machine needle and fine silk pins or ballpoint pins to avoid snagging. To finish narrow seams, use an overedge presser foot and a zigzag stitch. For straight or fine zigzag stitching, use a narrow-hole throat plate to keep the fabric from poking through the hole. Use narrow coil zippers.	Support the fabric with both hands as it feeds through the machine. If stitches skip, check the stitch length; make sure the thread is the right size for the needle. Make sure the needle is not clogged and the point is clean. Use tissue paper under the fabric to keep it from getting caught by the machine when making buttonholes and zigzag stitching.
Choose patterns that do not require facings, or eliminate extra bulk at edges by either of two alternatives: make facings of thin lining fabric, or substitute ribbon binding or knitted edging for facings.	Use ribs or wales and an L-shaped square to establish a straight edge. Make tailor tacks extra long to accommodate the extra thickness of the fabric.	Use pins with large colored heads or T-shaped heads to keep them from slipping through the loops of the fabric.	To prevent loops from catching on the machine, wrap the presser foot prongs with transparent tape and place tissue paper under fabric. Press seams over toweling to avoid ridges.

Sewing crinkled and treated fabrics

The two types of rumple-resistant fabrics presented in this chart are almost as popular as knits for traveling clothes, but the advantages of each kind come from properties which are diametrically opposite. One type of fabric travels well because it is deliberately crinkled and additional wrinkles do not show; the other has been given chemical finishes that counteract the fabric's natural tendency to wrinkle. Many of the special finishes also incorporate another travel bonus: they make the fabric more soil resistant.

The very attributes that make the treated and crinkled fabrics so good for traveling can, however, raise problems for the home seamstress. Crinkled fabrics, for example, do not flow as smoothly under the needle of the sewing machine; chemical finishes often fix the structure of a piece of cloth, making it impossible to straighten the grain by conventional methods. The chart at right is designed to pinpoint such problems and provide solutions that will simplify the task of shaping these fabrics into carefree separates for mussproof travel.

CRINKLED FABRICS

Some crinkled fabrics used for separates, like Indian mummy cloth, are made from naturally creped yarns that are crimped or twisted in the spinning process. Others are crinkled artificially, either by applying heat or chemical treatments in the finishing process or by manipulating the tension of the yarn while weaving. Most artificially crinkled fabrics are cotton or cotton-polyester blends such as seersucker, plissé, imitation mummy cloth or permanently wrinkled denim. But the crumpled appearance of crushed velvet is also achieved artificially, and so are the allover minuscule pleats that pattern the surface of some satins and crepes.

WRINKLE-SHEDDING FABRICS

Like the synthetics and blends, whose easy-care properties they emulate, these treated natural fabrics resist creasing and wrinkling and require little or no ironing. They are labeled variously as wrinkle resistant, crease resistant, wash-and-wear, drip-dry, permanent press or durable press. The finish itself is usually a synthetic resin applied during the last stages of manufacture; some types impregnate the fibers, while others coat the surface. Most often used on cottons, the finish may lessen the fabric's absorbency and make its surface smoother and harder than it is in its natural, untreated state.

PATTERN SELECTION	FABRIC HANDLING	ACCESSORIES	SEWING TIPS
For heavy fabrics, choose simple styles with few details, so as not to detract from the surface interest of the crinkle. For lighter fabrics, loose-fitting styles that feature draped effects are good, since the crinkle often makes the fabric fall in soft folds or cling to the body. Gathers and soft pleats work well in lightweight crinkled fabrics, and so do elastic and drawstring closures. Avoid close-fitting styles, which may destroy the characteristics of the fabric.	Preshrinking is very important, for washing or dry cleaning may accentuate the crinkle and affect the way the garment looks, making it, for instance, more form fitting. Crinkled fabrics should be pressed lightly and carefully, if at all, for their surfaces may be distorted or even smoothed out completely. However, the fabrics may have to be flattened somewhat, to facilitate laying out the pattern. To flatten, steam lightly with the iron held just above the surface, then smooth by hand.	Quick-drying elastics and tapes are useful for wash-and-wear versions of these fabrics. Do not use fusible interfacing or webbing, which flattens the crinkles. Even regular interfacing should be used only where absolutely necessary, as in collars and cuffs. Avoid trimmings with straight edges, such as ribbon, since they are difficult to attach evenly to crinkled surfaces.	Whether basting or sewing, do not stretch crinkled fabrics or pull them taut, lest you spoil their appearance. Instead, hold them loosely and ease in the fullness created by the crinkles. If the fabric tends to fray, make flat felled seams or finish the edges with overcast or zigzag stitching. Press seams only with the tip of the iron, to avoid flattening the surrounding fabric—or press the seams on the rounded surface of a pressing roll, or steam without pressing, and smooth the seam flat by hand.
The best styles are those with the least seaming or shaping because they pack flat and, when drip-dried, dry flat. Styles based on separates are especially easy to pack because they require less folding. Look for flared styles, since their diagonal seams pucker less than straight ones. Avoid styles such as set-in sleeves and other classic tailoring details that must be eased by shrinking and steaming. Treated fabrics are less pliant and cannot be readily eased. Topstitching at edges is a useful detail, since it helps compensate for the difficulty of pressing sharp creases in these fabrics.	Preshrink as for untreated fabric of the same type. Also preshrink all trims, notions and woven interfacings because treated fabrics are not flexible enough to adapt to slight changes in the dimensions of these materials. If the fabric comes from the bolt folded, check to make sure the fold can be removed by pressing; if it cannot, avoid placing pattern pieces across it. If the crosswise grain is not perpendicular to the lengthwise grain, ignore the usual grain-straightening techniques, which will not work on coated fabrics. Instead, align the pattern with the lengthwise grain or, if the fabric has a crosswise stripe, align the pattern with the stripe. The finished garment will usually hang properly even if it is cut off-grain, since treated fabrics have a very stable structure.	Use ballpoint needles, which help to eliminate puckered seams and which also do not pierce and break the resin-treated fibers. Keep an emery or conditioning pad handy to clean needles of sticky residues. Polyester thread, because of its greater strength and stretch, is recommended for these hard-finished fabrics. Use supersharp scissors, or have ordinary scissors sharpened more often. If using fusible webbing or interfacing, test it on a scrap of the fabric; generally, any fabric that can be steam-pressed without damage for 10 seconds is suitable for fusing. A presser foot that supplies additional control (pages 44-45) will minimize puckered seams by keeping fabric layers feeding evenly through the machine.	Needles should be changed more often than when sewing with untreated fabrics, because the resin-impregnated fibers dull them faster. Polyester thread, recommended for these fabrics, leaves a residue on machine parts; all parts touched by the thread should be cleaned frequently with a brush or cloth, but not with oil.

The crucial prelude for knits: cutting

The texture and design of a knit fabric can affect how it should be handled. A knit that is thick and spongy may be so resilient that the tracing wheel used over dressmaker's carbon cannot make an impression on the fabric to mark a clear seam line; on such material, straight seams must be achieved by using either the seam allowance gauge on the sewing machine or a seam guide attachment.

Knits also need special treatment before they can be cut to a pattern. Like all fabrics, they must first be straightened and smoothed—the edges evened and any creases flattened—but ordinary methods do not always work with knits. In synthetics and synthetic blends, for example, the direction of the yarns is fixed so that pulling, pressing and steaming, which straighten most woven textiles, have little effect—the yarns spring back to their original position, displaying the resilience that makes knits so useful. To get around this problem, assure straight edges on such knits by trimming along and at right angles to the ribs or stripes of the pattern (right); lay out pattern pieces to bypass any center crease and to align with any stripes.

TESTING KNITS FOR STRETCH

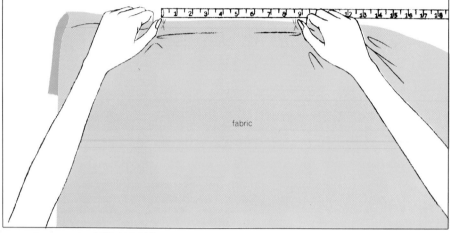

1. In an area of fabric that is at least 6 inches in from any of the edges, measure a 6-inch section along the crosswise grain. Mark each end of the section with a tailor tack (Appendix).

2. Grasp the fabric between thumb and forefinger near each tailor tack, and stretch the section as far as you can easily without twisting the fabric out of shape. Measure the stretched section by holding it against the ruler.

3. If the 6-inch section stretches to 7 inches or less, the fabric is a relatively stable knit; if it stretches to between 7 and 8 1/2 inches, it has moderate stretch; if the fabric stretches to more than 8 1/2 inches, it is very stretchy.

PREPARING KNIT FABRIC

1. Preshrink the fabric if necessary (see chart, pages 30-31).

2. For a very stretchy knit, spread the fabric out on a large flat surface and let it "relax" and flatten for at least a few hours before cutting and marking it.

3. If the fabric is tubular, cut it open along a lengthwise crease, following a rib or a stripe in the fabric so the lengthwise cut edges will be straight. Skip to Step 6.

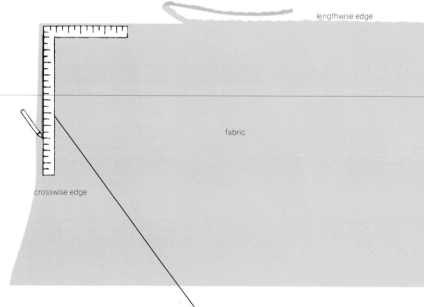

4. If the fabric has straight selvagelike edges, skip to Step 6.

5. If the fabric is not tubular and does not have straight selvagelike edges, straighten the lengthwise edges by trimming them along a rib, chain of stitches, or stripe.

6. To straighten the remaining edges, use an L-shaped square to draw a chalk line at a right angle to the straight edges. If the knit is too soft to mark with chalk, use pin markers.

7. Trim the edges along the marking.

8. If the fabric does not have a lengthwise rib or stripe that can be seen easily when laying out the pattern, find a narrow rib or chain of stitches just inside each lengthwise edge and baste along it. These bastings will serve as a guide for positioning the pattern pieces.

LAYING OUT KNIT FABRIC WITH A CENTER CREASE

1. To avoid the permanent center crease caused by folding the fabric onto the bolt, fold up both lengthwise edges, wrong sides out, so they meet near the crease. Keep the folds parallel to the bastings made in preparing knit fabric (opposite page). Fold up excess fabric so it will not hang over the edge of your work surface.

2. Lay the pattern pieces on the fabric. Be sure the top-to-bottom directions of all pieces are the same, grain-line arrows are parallel to the bastings and pieces marked "place on fold" are along a fold. Pin the pattern pieces.

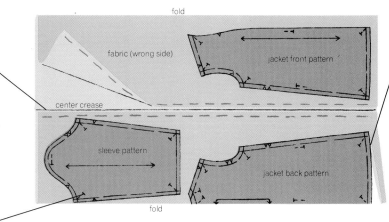

3. Cut out the garment pieces along the cutting lines.

4A. If the knit fabric is firm, mark each garment piece using dressmaker's carbon and a smooth-edged tracing wheel (pages 44-45).

4B. If the fabric is too soft to mark with carbon, mark all circles, dots and critical junctures of seam lines with single tailor tacks (Appendix). When you sew, use the seam guide on your sewing machine to assure straight seams.

LAYING OUT KNIT FABRIC WITH A PROMINENT LENGTHWISE RIB

1. Spread the fabric wrong side down in a single layer. Fold up excess fabric so it will not hang over the edge of your work surface.

2. Lay the pattern pieces on the fabric, avoiding creases; make sure all top-to-bottom directions are the same.

3. On pattern pieces marked "place on fold," align the fold line with a rib and leave space so each piece can be flipped, as shown by the dotted lines. Pin.

4. On all other pieces, align the grain-line arrow with a rib; leave space so pieces can be used a second time (dotted lines). Pin.

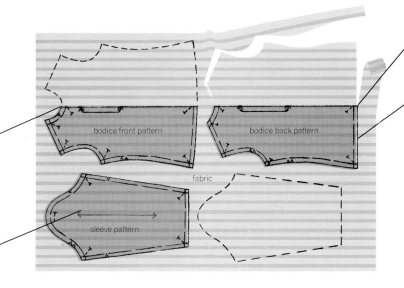

5. For a pattern piece with a fold line, cut first along the cutting lines to each end of the rib at the fold line.

6. Unpin the pattern. Turn the piece over with the fold line at the same rib. Repin and finish cutting.

7. For a pattern piece with a grain-line arrow, cut it out marked side up. Unpin and turn the piece over.

8. Repin the piece to the fabric with the same top-to-bottom directions previously used. Then cut the piece.

9. On each piece, mark dots, circles and critical junctures of seam lines with single tailor tacks (Appendix).

LAYING OUT KNIT FABRIC WITH A CROSSWISE STRIPE

1. Make a duplicate for all pattern pieces (Appendix).

2. Spread the fabric wrong side down in a single layer. Fold up excess fabric so it will not hang over the edge of your work surface.

3. Arrange the pattern pieces on the fabric, avoiding any creases present in the fabric, and make sure top-to-bottom directions on all pieces are the same. Grain-line arrows and fold lines are at right angles to the stripes. Pin the pattern pieces in place.

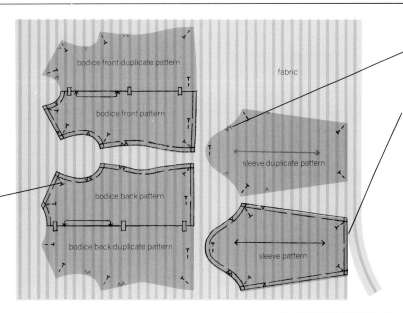

4. On adjacent garment pieces, be sure notches with the same numbers fall at the same points on the striped design so you can match stripes at seams.

5. Cut out the pieces along the cutting lines.

6. If the knit fabric is firm, transfer all pattern markings —including seam lines—to each garment piece with dressmaker's carbon and a smooth-edged tracing wheel.

7. If the fabric is too soft to mark with carbon, mark dots, circles and critical junctures of seam lines with tailor tacks (Appendix).

The Missonis, couturiers of knitwear

For Rosita Missoni, partner with her husband Ottavio in the enormously successful Italian knitwear factory that bears their name, clothes have no season. "When it is cool," says Signora Missoni, "you just put on more things," and the status-laden Missoni "things"—a running collection of knitted separates—are designed with that philosophy in mind. Wealthy women have been known to collect Missonis as they once collected cashmeres and wear them constantly. "You put three outfits in a suitcase and you're set for a whole season in Europe," said one Missoni admirer. "You just reach into your closet and grab—everything goes with everything else."

The particular cachet of the Missoni look is a combination of exotic and beautiful color effects achieved through a technique the Missonis call "space-dyeing," and a fashion sense that stresses easy effortless styles that are at once elegant and seductively sexy. Both the Missonis, whose factory lies in the foothills of the Alps about an hour's drive north of Milan, share in the creation of this distinctive look.

In the cobbled courtyard of their factory (right), Rosita and Ottavio Missoni pose a model in a four-part outfit: a rib-stitched skirt and sweater topped by a striped tunic and long woolen coat lined in the tunic fabric.

Sunburst stripes widening from top to bottom create a cotton knit beach skirt for a bikini (left). The bikini bra, which looks gathered, is actually the very top of the fabric pattern, where the narrowing stripes converge. Below, Rosita Missoni checks the look of a multistriped wrapped top worn over the same beach skirt. The head scarf, also a Missoni knit, doubles as a cummerbund.

37

In her office, next door to that of her husband, Rosita Missoni and her head cutter, Ersilia, check out a kingfisher-striped evening gown newly delivered from the production line, while Rosita's assistant Linda, in a Missoni man's shirt, takes notes on their comments. At right, Rosita and Linda pore over yarn samples on her floor and play an abstract game of color combinations, adding and subtracting until they have a palette for the 25 fabrics the Missonis create twice a year.

In the loose division of responsibility that exists between the two Missonis in their knitwear business, it is Ottavio who supervises the technical aspects—the knitting techniques and yarn combinations—while Rosita works with color and style. Her role as stylist begins when, as she puts it, Ottavio "delivers to me 10 meters of newly designed fabric." Her clothes are basically simple in shape, almost sacklike, but she has a special talent for putting together in one outfit extraordinary mixtures of patterns—zigzags, plaids and blurred stripes.

Standing by a knitting machine with his assistant Mariangela, Ottavio Missoni *(below)* discusses a fabric-in-process that may combine such disparate yarns as delicate mohair, tough nylon and sleek rayon.

3
PUTTING THE PARTS TOGETHER

One of the innovations of the space age is a machine that "sews" synthetic fabrics using neither needle nor thread. In place of the arm of a conventional sewing machine, it has a sonic horn that emits sound signals so high-pitched they are inaudible. These high-frequency vibrations generate localized heat in the fabric passing underneath it, liquefying the synthetic fibers and welding the two pieces into one.

TECHNIQUES AS ADVANCED AS THE TEXTILES

Although it will be a long time, if ever, before this machine is adapted to domestic use—among other things, the seam cannot be ripped out once made—the kind of man-made fabrics for which it was designed are already part of the home seamstress' repertoire. In fact, she can already sew many of these fabrics without needle and thread. The new fusible webs enable her to heat-seal, instead of stitching. The web, placed under the inside edge of a hem or seam allowance and steam pressed, welds a flexible and durable finish.

The fusibles, which are also made as interfacings, were developed to meet some of the problems created by the hundreds of man-made and knitted fabrics that, since their appearance in the decades following World War II, have become the basis of every travel wardrobe. Accustomed to working with natural woven fabrics, home seamstresses found these new fabrics difficult to sew with traditional techniques. Seams puckered, thread broke, the sewing machine skipped stitches.

Although a variety of factors contributed to these sewing problems, they all grew out of the nature of the materials. Synthetic yarns are much stronger than natural yarns; knitted cloth is much denser than woven cloth and its looped construction gives it a springy quality that older sewing equipment was not designed to handle. This strength and density cause dropped stitches by preventing the traditional sharp-pointed needle from penetrating the fabric to link up with the bobbin thread at just the right moment and angle. In the synthetics, the needle may stick in the fiber or be deflected by it. In knits, the needle may push the fabric into the throat plate and cause the stitches to miss. With the new ballpoint needles, which slide easily between the fibers instead of piercing them, these problems are now much reduced. The needles also help prevent puckered seams by seeking out the normal interstices in the cloth instead of forcing their way through the fiber and pushing it out of alignment.

But more than the correct needle is needed to prevent puckers in knits and synthetics. Cotton thread, for example, may fail to stretch as much as the fabric in sewing, and may shrink disproportionately in washing. It was to deal with these problems that the stretchable synthetic threads, cotton-and-polyester or pure polyester, were developed. Seams also pucker if sewing machine parts are not designed to deal with the slipperiness of synthetics or the resilience of knits. When the needle presses down on a knit, it may force the fabric into the hole in the throat plate, tangling it, since there is no resistance from surrounding stitches to hold the fabric taut. Also, when two layers of man-made fabric are fed through the machine, the upper layer slides under the smooth surface of the presser foot faster than the underlayer, which is held by the feed. To solve these problems, new presser feet have teeth or rollers to hold fabric firm, and a throat plate with a small hole keeps knits out of the bobbin area.

The special requirements of the new fabric have also forced the development of new techniques for making hems, seams and buttonholes (following pages). Indeed, the very qualities that make the new knits so difficult to sew inspired New York designer Stephen Burrows to create a new type of hem that has become his trademark. This "lettuce hem," a wavy, fluttery-edge finish (page 87), is produced by stretching the knit while sewing a narrow zigzag stitch. For Burrows, as for many who sew at home, the new fabrics have turned out to be not limiting, but liberating.

Under the iron lie woven and nonwoven interfacing, and a gossamer webbing for bonding fabrics together, all three fused by heat and particularly useful for making packable separates. Below the lightweight nylon snaps are fast-drying elastics; the center two have nonrolling edges. At bottom are four extremely trim zippers with nonshrinking polyester tapes.

Machine accessories for stretchy or slippery fabrics include presser feet (top) and a throat plate with a small hole (to keep knits from poking through the plate). The two top feet give extra control in feeding fabric evenly; the overedge foot below them keeps narrow zigzag seams on knits from curling. The smooth tracing wheel (top) marks more visibly on knits. Below the supersharp scissors are an emery and a conditioning pad to smooth needles.

New tools for sewing new materials

The qualities of toughness, washability and wrinkle resistance that make new man-made fabrics and knits suitable for a travel wardrobe also present a range of new problems for the home seamstress.

Synthetic fibers like nylon and polyester are so strong they tend to blunt sewing tools. To cope, special pins, needles and scissors have been developed along with needle-sharpening devices. Since the fabrics are also slippery and the knits springy, they require new machine feet, designed to apply even pressure and ensure that the fabrics pass smoothly under the needle.

Sewing notions, too, have been developed to go with the fabrics. Elastics, zippers and even snaps are now made in super-lightweight, fast-drying versions. And fusible interfacings and webs provide a quick way to shape garments, anchor hems and reinforce seams, particularly on nonwoven pseudo suedes.

In this magnified photograph, the wedge-point needle *(near left)* sews coated fabrics, leather and pseudo suedes. The ballpoint needle next to it, like the ballpoint pins above, slips easily between the threads of knits and man-made fabrics, rather than piercing the fibers.

Foolproof zippers and buttonholes

Closures for nonwoven fabrics used in many travel separates have always been something of a problem. Zippers on knit garments are often placed where there are no seams; in both knits and pseudo suedes, bound buttonholes can be bulky and difficult to align. Now there are ways around such obstacles.

The plastic zipper in the mock turtle top is inserted in a slash faced with a strip of lining fabric, thus making the edge easier to stitch. For double knits and pseudo suedes, there are two foolproof buttonhole techniques. The one for double-faced pseudo suede uses fusible web to hold buttonhole parts in place for stitching.

THE EXPOSED ZIPPER FOR A DOUBLE-LAYERED RIBBED COLLAR

A | PREPARING THE GARMENT AND THE LINING

1. With the garment right side out, draw a chalk placement line for the zipper opening down the center back or center front from the top edge of the ribbed collar to just below the bottom of the armholes.

2. To mark the location of the top zipper stop, measure the collar from the top edge to the neck seam. Divide this figure in half and add 1/4 inch. Then mark the center line at this distance from the top edge of the collar.

3. Using a lightweight woven lining fabric of the garment color, cut a strip 2 inches wide and the length of the zipper plus 2 inches.

4. Draw a pencil line down the center of the lining strip.

5. To mark the zipper seam lines on the lining, draw lines the length of the zipper parallel to the center line. For a lightweight zipper, draw the lines 1/8 inch from the center line; for a heavyweight decorative zipper, draw the lines 3/16 inch from the center line. Connect the bottom ends of these two lines.

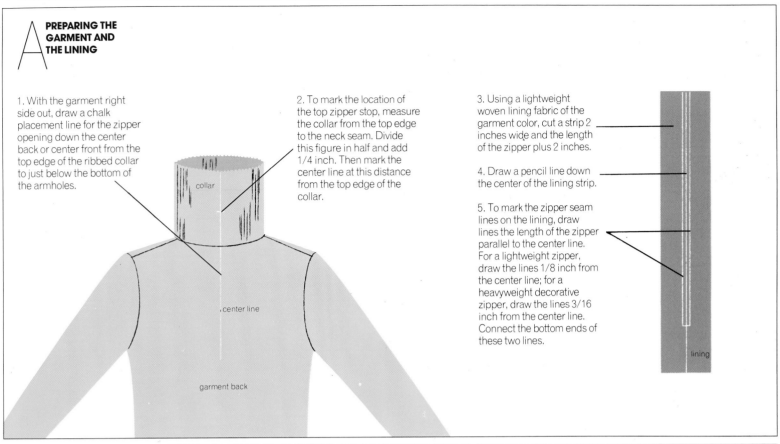

B | ATTACHING THE LINING STRIP

6. Place the lining strip, marked side up, on the garment. Match the center lines and align the top edge of the lining with the mark on the collar made in Step 2. Pin.

7. Baste the lining to the garment on the center line. Remove the pins.

8. Extend the zipper seam-line markings (Step 5) to the top of the collar. Machine stitch around the zipper seam-line markings on the collar and lining, pivoting at the bottom corners. Remove the basting.

9. Cut through all layers of fabric along the center line to within 1/2 inch of the bottom of the stitching made in Step 8. Then clip the bottom corners diagonally, cutting up to but not into the stitching.

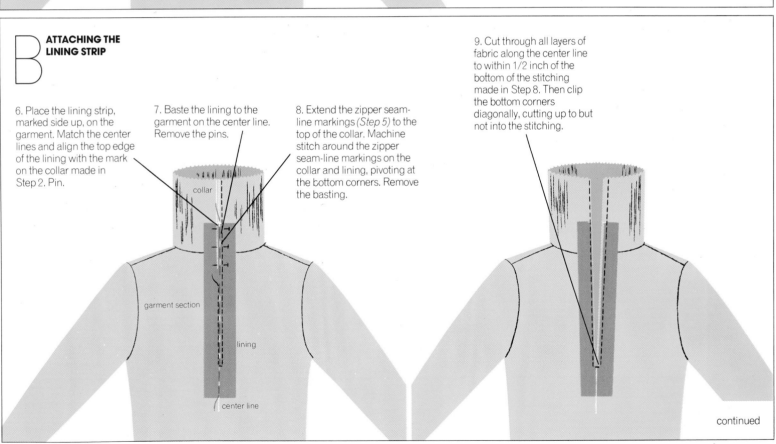

continued

ATTACHING THE ZIPPER

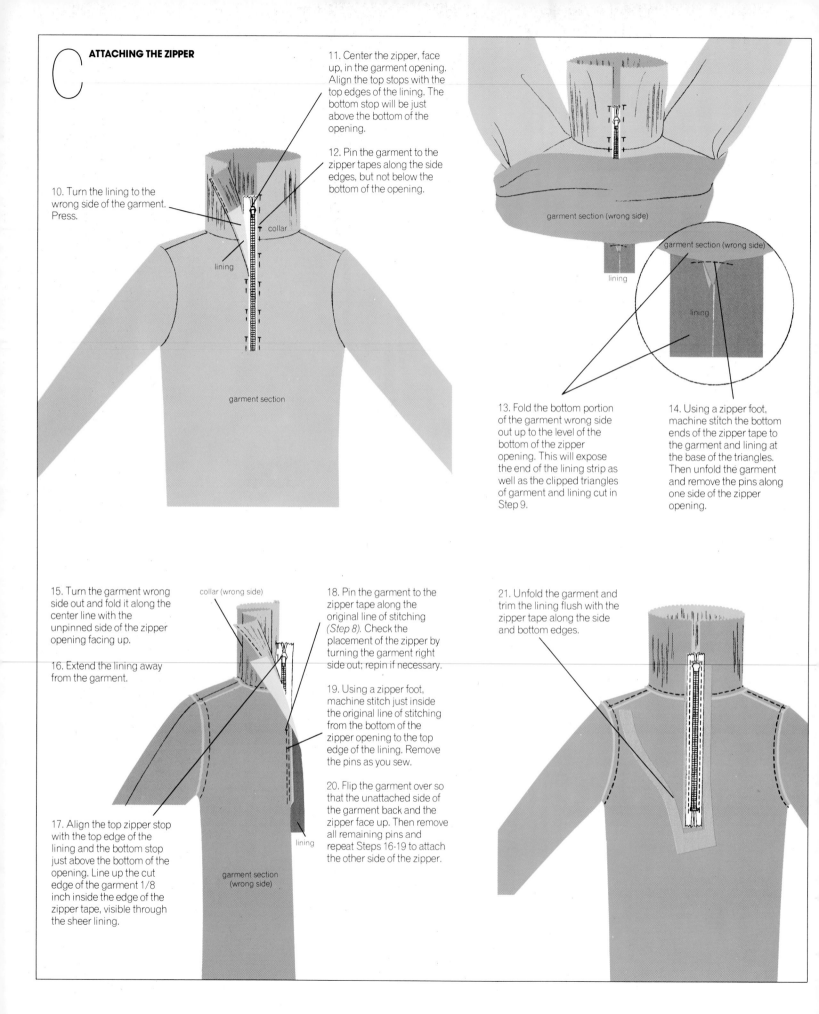

10. Turn the lining to the wrong side of the garment. Press.

11. Center the zipper, face up, in the garment opening. Align the top stops with the top edges of the lining. The bottom stop will be just above the bottom of the opening.

12. Pin the garment to the zipper tapes along the side edges, but not below the bottom of the opening.

garment section

collar

lining

garment section (wrong side)

lining

garment section (wrong side)

lining

13. Fold the bottom portion of the garment wrong side out up to the level of the bottom of the zipper opening. This will expose the end of the lining strip as well as the clipped triangles of garment and lining cut in Step 9.

14. Using a zipper foot, machine stitch the bottom ends of the zipper tape to the garment and lining at the base of the triangles. Then unfold the garment and remove the pins along one side of the zipper opening.

15. Turn the garment wrong side out and fold it along the center line with the unpinned side of the zipper opening facing up.

16. Extend the lining away from the garment.

17. Align the top zipper stop with the top edge of the lining and the bottom stop just above the bottom of the opening. Line up the cut edge of the garment 1/8 inch inside the edge of the zipper tape, visible through the sheer lining.

collar (wrong side)

lining

garment section (wrong side)

18. Pin the garment to the zipper tape along the original line of stitching *(Step 8)*. Check the placement of the zipper by turning the garment right side out; repin if necessary.

19. Using a zipper foot, machine stitch just inside the original line of stitching from the bottom of the zipper opening to the top edge of the lining. Remove the pins as you sew.

20. Flip the garment over so that the unattached side of the garment back and the zipper face up. Then remove all remaining pins and repeat Steps 16-19 to attach the other side of the zipper.

21. Unfold the garment and trim the lining flush with the zipper tape along the side and bottom edges.

22. Turn the garment right side out and open the zipper.

23. Along one edge of the zipper opening, extend the zipper tape away from the garment to flip that edge of the zipper wrong side out.

24. Fold down diagonally the unattached top end of the zipper tape, extending it away from the garment. Pin.

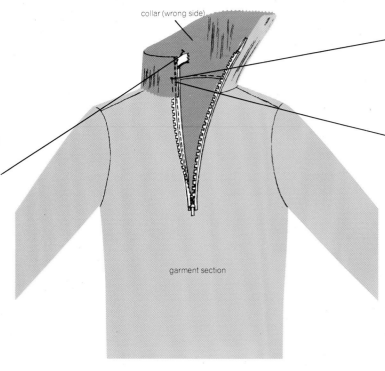

collar (wrong side)

garment section

25. Fold down the collar above the top zipper stop and align the cut edge 1/8 inch inside the edge of the zipper tape. The bottom edge of the collar should extend 1/4 inch beyond the neck seam. Pin.

26. Machine stitch the collar to the zipper tape along the line of stitching made in Step 8, removing the pins as you sew.

27. Repeat Steps 23-26 to attach the other side of the collar.

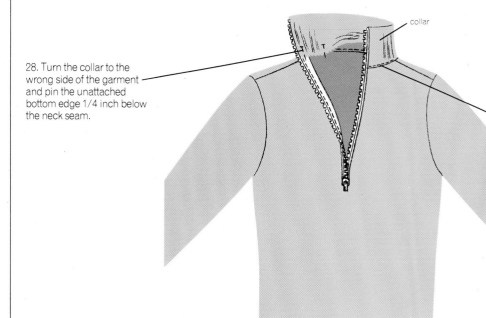

collar

28. Turn the collar to the wrong side of the garment and pin the unattached bottom edge 1/4 inch below the neck seam.

29. Attach the bottom edge of the collar to the garment with machine stitching or loose backstitches, stretching the fabric as you sew. Stitch from the finished side of the garment in the groove formed by the neck seam. Remove the pins.

A PREPARING THE GARMENT AND THE INTERFACING

1. Place the right-front garment section wrong side up.

2. To determine the width for the buttonholes, measure the diameter and thickness of your button and add the two figures.

3. Mark a guide for the outer edge of the buttonholes by drawing a pencil or chalk line down the garment 1/8 inch outside and parallel to the center-front line.

4. Using the width found in Step 2, mark a guide for the inner edge of the buttonholes by drawing a line inside and parallel to the line made in Step 3.

5. Using your paper pattern as a guide for the number and spacing of the buttonholes, mark a horizontal center line for each buttonhole between, and perpendicular to, the two vertical lines drawn in Steps 3 and 4.

6. To mark the top and bottom edges of each buttonhole, draw two horizontal lines 1/8 inch on either side of the center lines marked in Step 5.

7. Cut out each buttonhole rectangle along the markings with a razor-edged knife, using a ruler as a guide.

8. Using lightweight nonwoven fusible interfacing, cut out and mark interfacing pieces for the neckline and front opening. If your pattern does not provide for an interfacing, use the facing pattern piece, then trim away 3/8 inch from the long unmarked edge.

9. Place the right-front interfacing fusible side down.

10. Mark the vertical and horizontal placement lines for the buttonholes as shown in Steps 3-6.

11. Cut out each buttonhole rectangle 1/8 inch outside the markings.

12. Place the right-front interfacing, marked side up, on the wrong side of the right-front garment section. Match the vertical buttonhole markings and center the cutout buttonhole rectangles of the interfacing around the buttonhole cutouts of the fabric.

13. Fuse the interfacing to the garment with an iron following the directions on the package.

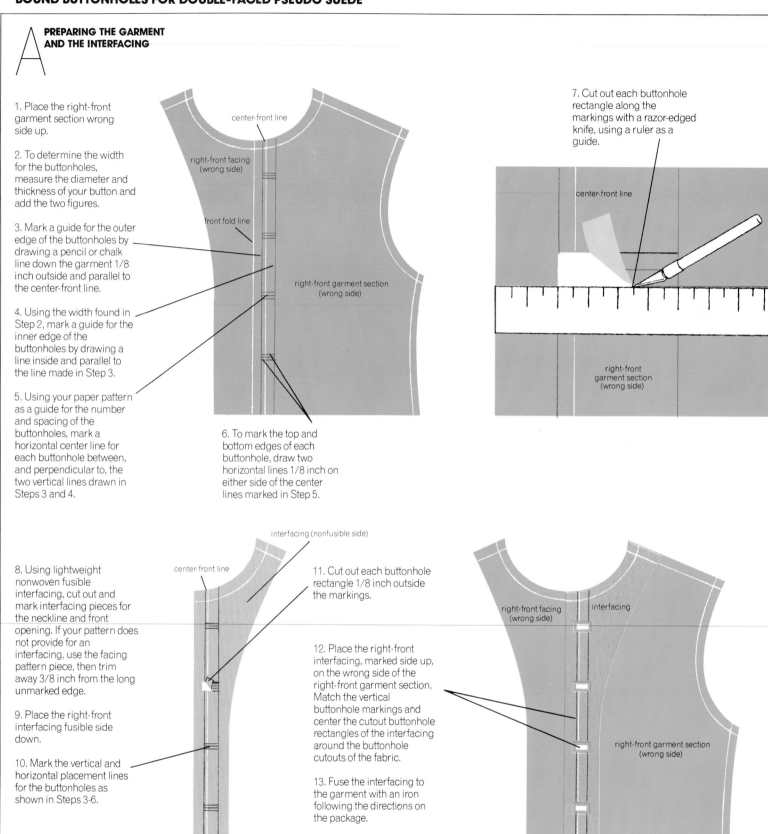

**PREPARING AND
ATTACHING THE LIPS OF
THE BUTTONHOLES**

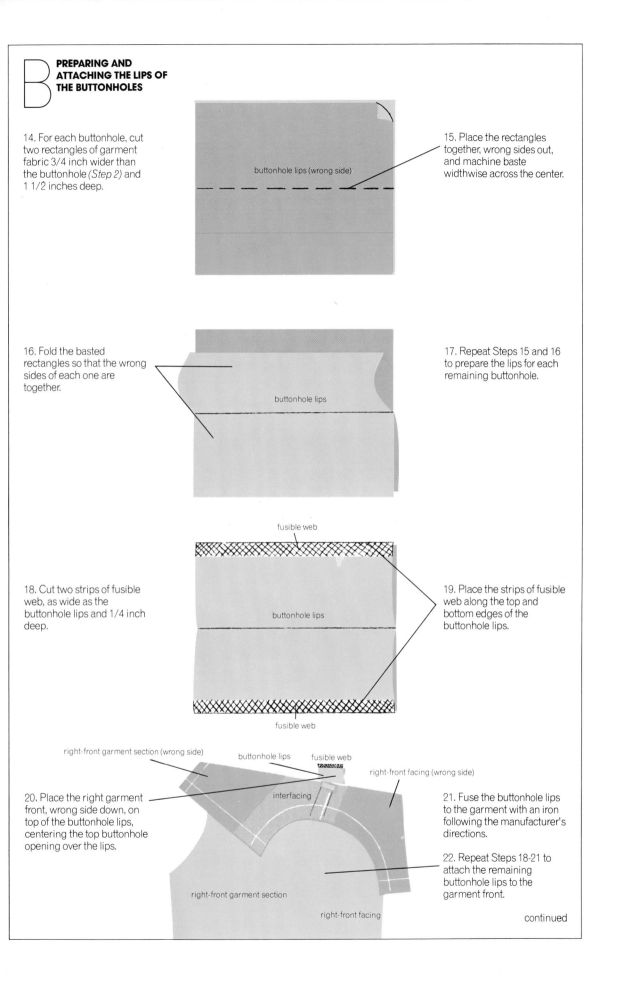

14. For each buttonhole, cut two rectangles of garment fabric 3/4 inch wider than the buttonhole *(Step 2)* and 1 1/2 inches deep.

buttonhole lips *(wrong side)*

15. Place the rectangles together, wrong sides out, and machine baste widthwise across the center.

16. Fold the basted rectangles so that the wrong sides of each one are together.

buttonhole lips

17. Repeat Steps 15 and 16 to prepare the lips for each remaining buttonhole.

fusible web

18. Cut two strips of fusible web, as wide as the buttonhole lips and 1/4 inch deep.

buttonhole lips

19. Place the strips of fusible web along the top and bottom edges of the buttonhole lips.

fusible web

right-front garment section *(wrong side)*   buttonhole lips   fusible web   right-front facing *(wrong side)*

interfacing

20. Place the right garment front, wrong side down, on top of the buttonhole lips, centering the top buttonhole opening over the lips.

right-front garment section

right-front facing

21. Fuse the buttonhole lips to the garment with an iron following the manufacturer's directions.

22. Repeat Steps 18-21 to attach the remaining buttonhole lips to the garment front.

continued

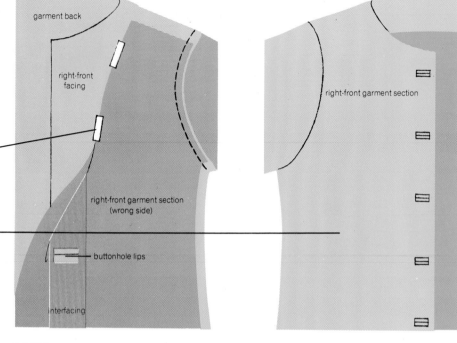

23. Before finishing the buttonholes, assemble the garment following the pattern instructions. Turn the facing to the wrong side and smooth it flat against the garment front.

24. To keep the facing of the right-front section from shifting, tape the long unattached edge to the garment with several strips of masking tape.

25. Turn the garment right side out.

26. Sewing from the finished side of the right-front garment section through all layers, machine stitch around the buttonhole opening 1/16 inch inside the cut edges of the garment fabric. Begin midway along one long edge and stitch to the corner.

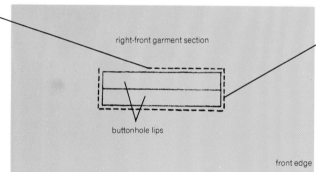

27. Pivot and stitch down the short edge to the corner, counting the stitches. Pivot and stitch along the other long edge. Pivot at the next corner; stitch along the second short edge, taking the same number of stitches as on the first short edge. Pivot; complete the line by stitching over the first few stitches made. Pull the threads through to the wrong side and clip.

28. Turn the garment wrong side up.

29. Using embroidery scissors, trim away the facing fabric inside the stitched rectangle. Cut close to but not into the stitching, taking care not to cut into the buttonhole lips.

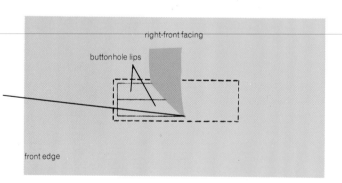

30. Turn the garment wrong side down.

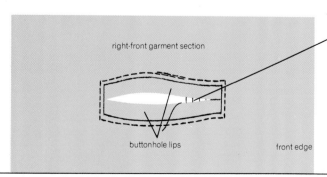

31. Using embroidery scissors, carefully clip the machine basting holding the buttonhole lips closed.

32. Repeat Steps 26-31 to complete the remaining buttonholes. Then remove the masking tape holding the facing in place.

BOUND BUTTONHOLES FOR DOUBLE KNITS

A PREPARING THE GARMENT AND THE INTERFACING

1. Cut out and mark the garment sections following your pattern instructions.

2. Cut out and mark interfacing pieces for the neckline and front opening. If your pattern does not provide for interfacing, use the facing pattern, then trim away 3/8 inch from the long unmarked edges.

3. Place the right-front garment section wrong side up and lay the right-front interfacing on top of it, matching the neck and shoulder seam-line markings. Align the front edge of the interfacing with the front fold-line marking on the garment. Pin.

4. Attach the interfacing to the garment along the front edge with a catch stitch (Appendix) using thread of the same color as the garment.

5. Baste the interfacing to the garment just outside the neck and shoulder seam-line markings and along the long unmarked edge. Remove the pins.

6. Determine the width of the buttonholes and mark guide lines for them on the interfacing as shown for bound buttonholes for pseudo suede (page 50, Steps 2-6).

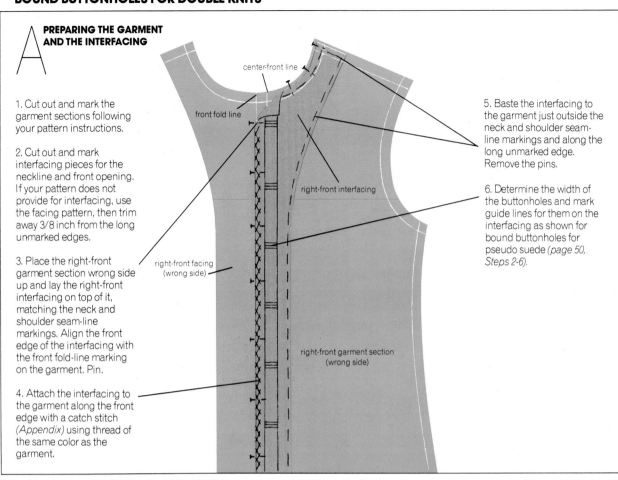

center-front line

front fold line

right-front interfacing

right-front facing (wrong side)

right-front garment section (wrong side)

B MAKING AND POSITIONING THE REINFORCEMENT PATCH

7. Using organza or lightweight lining material of the same color as the garment fabric, cut a reinforcement patch for each buttonhole 1 inch wider than the buttonhole and 2 inches deep.

8. Slip a patch underneath the right-front garment section so that the patch is centered under the top buttonhole marking.

9. Pin the patch to the garment fabric, inserting the pins from the wrong side of the garment.

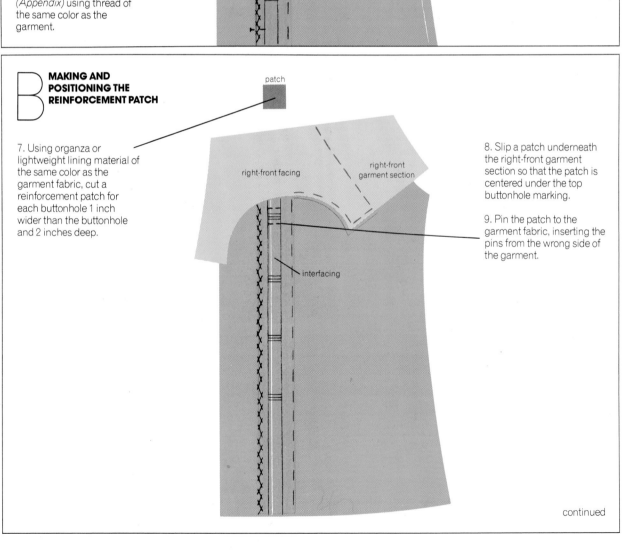

patch

right-front facing

right-front garment section

interfacing

continued

C ATTACHING THE REINFORCEMENT PATCH

10. Machine stitch—at 15 stitches to the inch—around the markings for the buttonhole opening. Begin midway along one long edge and stitch to the corner. Pivot and stitch to the next corner, counting the number of stitches taken along the short edge.

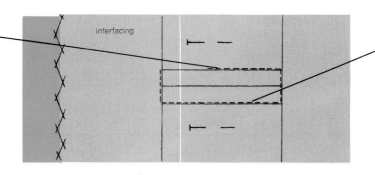

11. Pivot and stitch along the other long edge. Pivot at the next corner and stitch along the second short edge, taking the same number of stitches as on the first short edge. Pivot again and complete the line, stitching over the first few stitches made. Remove the pins.

12. Cutting through all layers, slash open the buttonhole along the center line. Cut to within 1/4 inch of each short end. Then clip into the corners diagonally, cutting up to but not into the stitching.

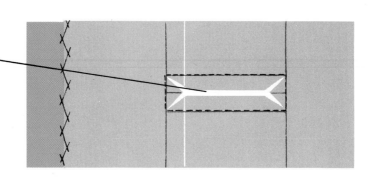

13. Pull the reinforcement patch through the opening to the wrong side of the garment. Push the seam allowances away from the opening and press.

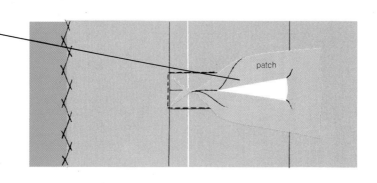

14. Repeat Steps 8-13 to attach a reinforcement patch to each remaining buttonhole.

D PREPARING THE LIPS OF THE BUTTONHOLES

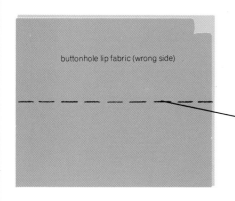

15. For each buttonhole, cut two rectangles of garment fabric 1 inch wider than the buttonhole and 2 inches deep.

16. Place the rectangles together, wrong sides out, and machine baste across the width at the center.

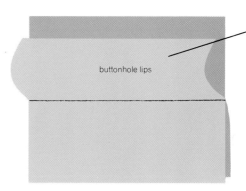

17. Fold the basted rectangles so the wrong sides are together.

18. Repeat Steps 16 and 17 to prepare the lips for each remaining buttonhole.

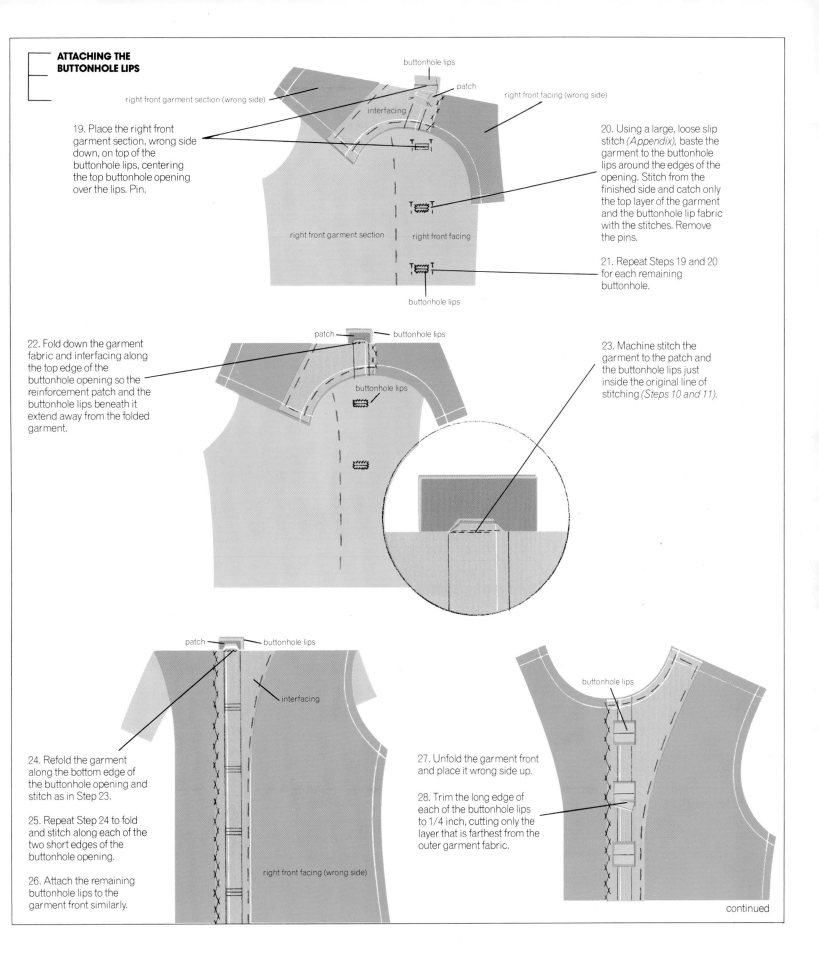

buttonhole lips

patch

right front garment section (wrong side)

right front facing (wrong side)

interfacing

19. Place the right front garment section, wrong side down, on top of the buttonhole lips, centering the top buttonhole opening over the lips. Pin.

20. Using a large, loose slip stitch (Appendix), baste the garment to the buttonhole lips around the edges of the opening. Stitch from the finished side and catch only the top layer of the garment and the buttonhole lip fabric with the stitches. Remove the pins.

right front garment section

right front facing

21. Repeat Steps 19 and 20 for each remaining buttonhole.

buttonhole lips

patch

buttonhole lips

22. Fold down the garment fabric and interfacing along the top edge of the buttonhole opening so the reinforcement patch and the buttonhole lips beneath it extend away from the folded garment.

buttonhole lips

23. Machine stitch the garment to the patch and the buttonhole lips just inside the original line of stitching (Steps 10 and 11).

patch

buttonhole lips

interfacing

buttonhole lips

24. Refold the garment along the bottom edge of the buttonhole opening and stitch as in Step 23.

25. Repeat Step 24 to fold and stitch along each of the two short edges of the buttonhole opening.

26. Attach the remaining buttonhole lips to the garment front similarly.

right front facing (wrong side)

27. Unfold the garment front and place it wrong side up.

28. Trim the long edge of each of the buttonhole lips to 1/4 inch, cutting only the layer that is farthest from the outer garment fabric.

continued

55

29. Before finishing the buttonholes, complete the garment following your pattern instructions. Then turn the garment right side out.

30. To keep the facing from shifting, baste around each buttonhole through all layers of the fabric.

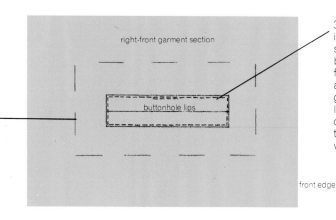

31. Following the directions in Steps 10 and 11, machine stitch around each buttonhole in the grooves formed by the seams attaching the lips to the garment. Sew through all layers from the finished side of the fabric. Then pull the threads through to the wrong side and clip.

32. Turn the garment wrong side out.

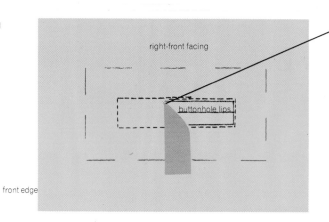

33. Using embroidery scissors, trim away the facing fabric inside the stitched buttonhole rectangles. Cut close to but not into the stitching, taking care not to cut into the buttonhole lips.

34. Turn the garment right side out.

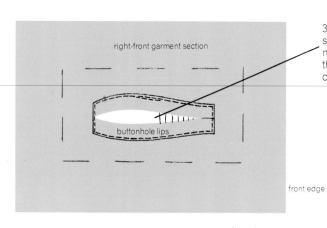

35. Using embroidery scissors, carefully clip the machine basting holding the lips of each buttonhole closed. Remove all bastings.

CORDED MACHINE-WORKED BUTTONHOLES FOR STRETCHABLE KNITS

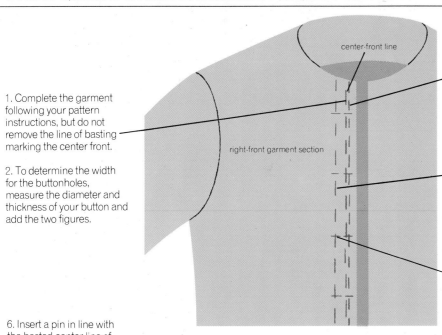

1. Complete the garment following your pattern instructions, but do not remove the line of basting marking the center front.

2. To determine the width for the buttonholes, measure the diameter and thickness of your button and add the two figures.

3. With the right-front garment section wrong side down, mark a guide for the outer edge of the buttonholes by basting a line of stitches 1/8 inch outside and parallel to the center-front line.

4. Using the buttonhole width determined in Step 2, mark a guide for the inner edge of the buttonhole by basting a line of stitches inside and parallel to the line made in Step 3.

5. Using your paper pattern as a guide for the number and spacing of the buttonholes, baste a horizontal center line for each buttonhole between and perpendicular to the two vertical lines of basting made in Steps 3 and 4.

6. Insert a pin in line with the basted center line of each buttonhole, 1 1/2 inches inside the inner buttonhole edge. The pin heads must face away from the buttonhole markings.

7. For each buttonhole, cut a 10-inch length of cording from buttonhole twist thread of the same color as your regular thread.

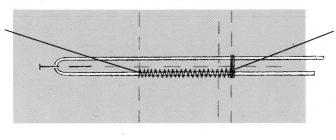

8. Fold one piece of the cording in half and place the loop around the head of one of the pins. Then arrange the cording parallel to, and above and below, the center-line marking of the buttonhole.

9. Holding the cording straight, run machine zigzag stitches on one side of the buttonhole over the cording, following the directions accompanying your machine. Sew from the inner edge marking (Step 3); do not sew into the cording.

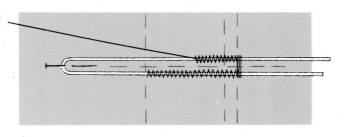

10. Make a bar tack at the outer edge of the buttonhole, sewing over but not into both the top and bottom parts of the cording.

11. Stitch the second side of the buttonhole, sewing over but not into the cording.

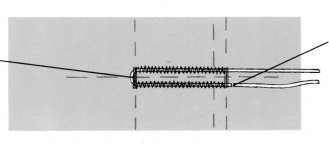

12. Finish the second end of the buttonhole with a bar tack, stitching over but not into both the top and bottom parts of the cording. Remove the pin.

13. Pull the cut ends of the cording until the loop is flush with the second bar tack. Clip the excess cording close to the first bar tack.

14. Repeat Steps 8-13 to work the remaining buttonholes.

Pockets for carrying things

Pockets are often decorative, but their primary purpose—to transport paraphernalia and leave the hands free—make them exceptionally welcome to travelers. They are especially so when they come in multiples, as on the shirt at right, and have such features as button-down flaps and a double row of stitching around the edge to protect the pocket's contents. Another less tailored pocket good for traveling is shown on pages 63-65. It is a gathered, roomy affair, lined for additional strength and held in shape across the top with an interfaced band.

THE PLEATED PATCH POCKET WITH FLAP

A MAKING THE POCKET AND FLAP PATTERNS

1. To make the paper pattern for a 4 1/2-inch-square breast pocket, draw a 4 1/2-by-7 1/2-inch rectangle. To make the paper pattern for a 6 1/2-inch-square hip pocket, draw a 6 1/2-by-10.1/2-inch rectangle. The top of this rectangle will be the top fold line of the pocket, the sides and bottom will be seam lines.

2. Draw three cutting lines 1/2 inch outside of and parallel to the seam lines. Then draw one cutting line 1 inch (1 1/2 inches for a hip pocket) above the top fold line.

3. Extend the top fold lines to the side cutting lines.

4. To mark the pleat, first draw outer pleating lines from the top to the bottom cutting lines 1 1/2 inches (2 1/4 inches for a hip pocket) in from each side seam line.

5. Divide the area between the outer pleating lines into thirds by drawing inner pleating lines 1 1/2 inches (2 1/4 inches for a hip pocket) in from each outer pleating line.

6. Cut out the pocket pattern along the cutting lines.

7. To make the paper pattern for the flap, draw the top seam line 1/4 inch longer than the finished size of the pocket (Step 1).

8. Draw side seam lines from the ends of the top seam line downward and perpendicular to it. Make each line 1/2 inch long (2 inches for a hip pocket).

9. Mark the bottom of the V-shaped edge midway from the side seams 2 1/2 inches (3 for a hip pocket) below the top seam line. Connect this mark with the lower end of each side seam line.

10. For a vertical buttonhole line, measure up from the lowest point of the V-shaped edge a distance equal to the radius of your button plus 1/4 inch, and mark. From this mark draw a line equal in length to the diameter of the button plus its thickness.

11. Draw cutting lines 1/2 inch outside of and parallel to each seam line.

12. Cut out the flap pattern along the cutting lines.

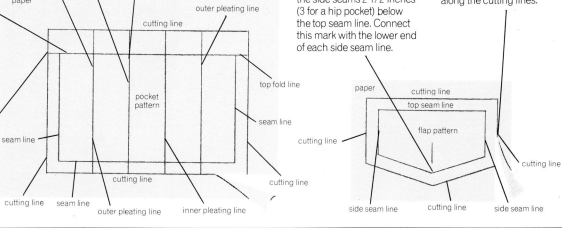

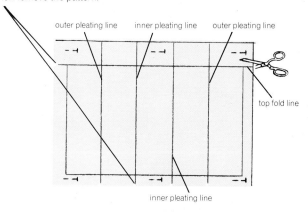

B CUTTING OUT AND MARKING THE POCKET AND FLAP PIECES

13. Lay the pocket fabric, wrong side up, on a flat surface. (To make two pockets, fold the fabric in half lengthwise, wrong sides out.)

14. Place the pocket pattern on the fabric, aligning the vertical side edges with the selvage or the lengthwise grain of the fabric. Pin.

15. Place the flap pattern on the fabric next, aligning the vertical side edges with the selvage. Insert pins inside the seam lines so that the lines can be traced onto the fabric without moving the pins.

16. Cut out the patterns. For each pocket, cut out two flap pieces, one to serve as the flap front and the other as the flap facing.

17. To mark the pocket fabric, make a 1/4-inch clip into both ends of each pleating line and the top fold line. Remove the pattern.

18. To mark the flap fabric, use a dressmaker's carbon and a tracing wheel to trace all lines—except the buttonhole line—to the wrong side of one of the flap pieces. The marked piece will be the flap front. Remove the pattern.

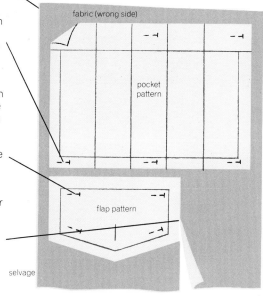

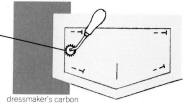

continued

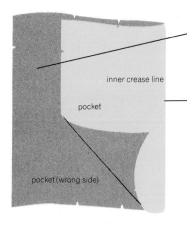

19. To make a box pleat in the pocket, place the fabric wrong side up.

20. Fold over one side of the pocket at the clip marks for the first inner pleating line and align the top and bottom edges of the fabric. Press in a crease along the fold.

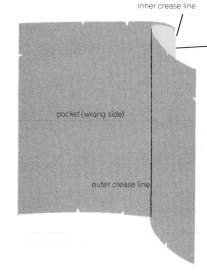

21. Fold the side of the pocket back until the clip marks for the first outer pleating line align with the crease made in the preceding step. Press in a crease along the fold to form the first half of the pleat.

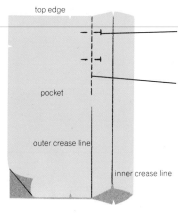

22. To complete the other half of the pleat, turn the pocket 180° and repeat Steps 20 and 21. Make sure the creases of the completed pleat meet exactly at the center of the pocket.

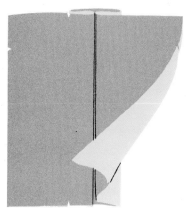

23. To stitch the pleat in place, first flip one side edge of the pocket across the pleat to the other side edge —thus folding the pocket in half with the wrong sides in.

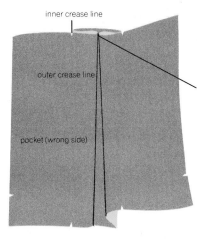

24. Align the edges and insert two pins near the top of the pleat at the outer creases (Step 21).

25. Starting from the top edge, machine stitch on the outer creases for 2 1/2 inches (3 1/2 inches for a hip pocket), removing the pins as you sew.

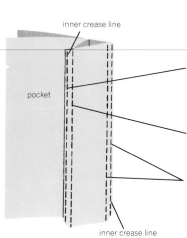

26. To stitch the inner creases of the box pleat (Step 20), first make a row of stitching close to one crease from the top to the bottom edges of the pocket.

27. Make a second row of stitching 1/4 inch inside the first row.

28. To stitch the other inner crease, repeat Steps 26 and 27, making sure to push away the rest of the piece from under the edge before you begin.

D FINISHING THE EDGES OF THE POCKET PIECE

29. Turn the pleated pocket wrong side up and place it on a flat surface.

30. To make the top hem, turn down the top edge 1/4 inch and press in a crease.

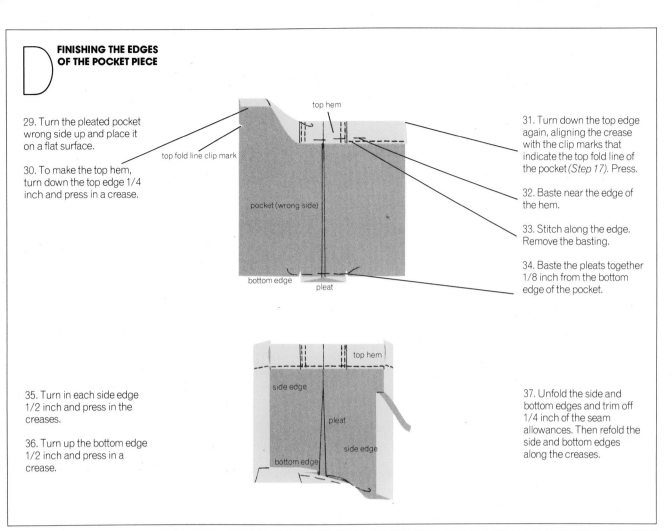

31. Turn down the top edge again, aligning the crease with the clip marks that indicate the top fold line of the pocket *(Step 17)*. Press.

32. Baste near the edge of the hem.

33. Stitch along the edge. Remove the basting.

34. Baste the pleats together 1/8 inch from the bottom edge of the pocket.

35. Turn in each side edge 1/2 inch and press in the creases.

36. Turn up the bottom edge 1/2 inch and press in a crease.

37. Unfold the side and bottom edges and trim off 1/4 inch of the seam allowances. Then refold the side and bottom edges along the creases.

E ATTACHING THE POCKET

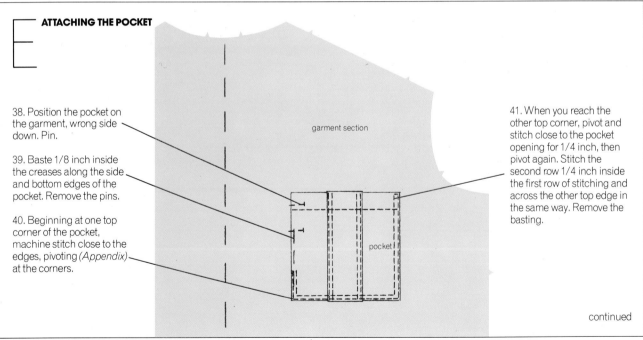

38. Position the pocket on the garment, wrong side down. Pin.

39. Baste 1/8 inch inside the creases along the side and bottom edges of the pocket. Remove the pins.

40. Beginning at one top corner of the pocket, machine stitch close to the edges, pivoting *(Appendix)* at the corners.

41. When you reach the other top corner, pivot and stitch close to the pocket opening for 1/4 inch, then pivot again. Stitch the second row 1/4 inch inside the first row of stitching and across the other top edge in the same way. Remove the basting.

continued

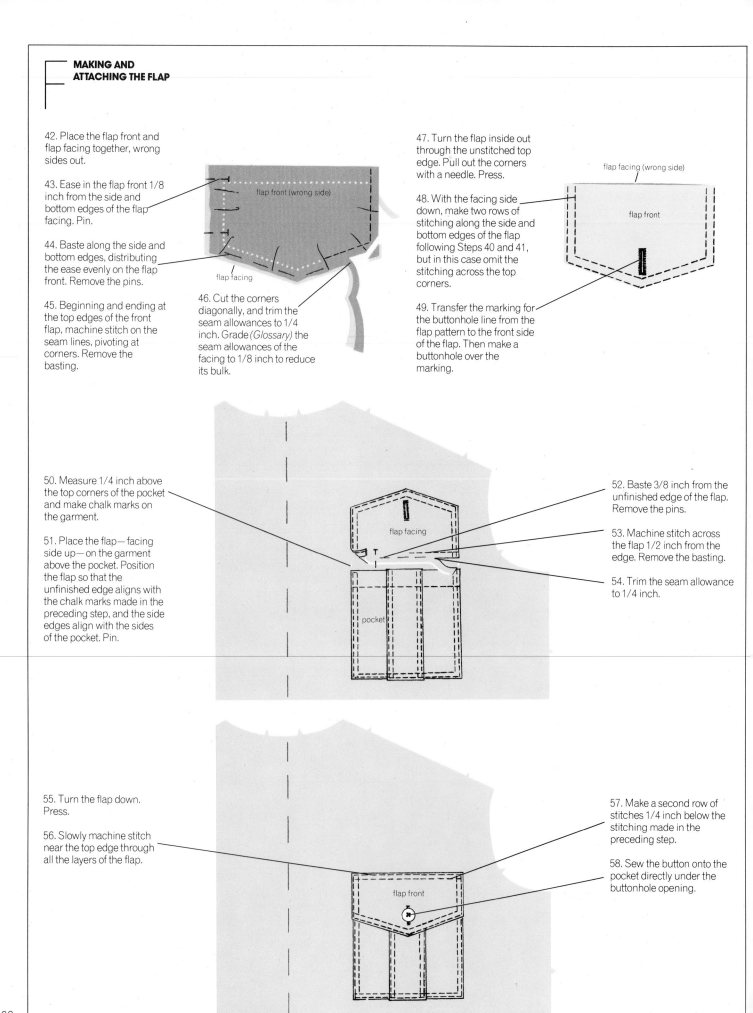

42. Place the flap front and flap facing together, wrong sides out.

43. Ease in the flap front 1/8 inch from the side and bottom edges of the flap facing. Pin.

44. Baste along the side and bottom edges, distributing the ease evenly on the flap front. Remove the pins.

45. Beginning and ending at the top edges of the front flap, machine stitch on the seam lines, pivoting at corners. Remove the basting.

46. Cut the corners diagonally, and trim the seam allowances to 1/4 inch. Grade (Glossary) the seam allowances of the facing to 1/8 inch to reduce its bulk.

flap front (wrong side)

flap facing

47. Turn the flap inside out through the unstitched top edge. Pull out the corners with a needle. Press.

48. With the facing side down, make two rows of stitching along the side and bottom edges of the flap following Steps 40 and 41, but in this case omit the stitching across the top corners.

49. Transfer the marking for the buttonhole line from the flap pattern to the front side of the flap. Then make a buttonhole over the marking.

flap facing (wrong side)

flap front

50. Measure 1/4 inch above the top corners of the pocket and make chalk marks on the garment.

51. Place the flap—facing side up—on the garment above the pocket. Position the flap so that the unfinished edge aligns with the chalk marks made in the preceding step, and the side edges align with the sides of the pocket. Pin.

flap facing

pocket

52. Baste 3/8 inch from the unfinished edge of the flap. Remove the pins.

53. Machine stitch across the flap 1/2 inch from the edge. Remove the basting.

54. Trim the seam allowance to 1/4 inch.

55. Turn the flap down. Press.

56. Slowly machine stitch near the top edge through all the layers of the flap.

flap front

57. Make a second row of stitches 1/4 inch below the stitching made in the preceding step.

58. Sew the button onto the pocket directly under the buttonhole opening.

THE GATHERED POCKET WITH BAND

A MAKING THE POCKET PATTERN

1. To make a paper pattern for a gathered pocket with a band at the top, draw a square the size you want the pocket to be at its widest point. The top of the square will be the top cutting line.

2. Widen the bottom of the pocket by extending the bottom line of the square 1/4 inch on each side.

3. Connect the ends of the extended bottom line to the top corners of the square. These diagonal lines will be the side cutting lines.

4. To round the bottom of the pocket, make a dot 1/4 inch below the mid-point of the bottom line of the square.

5. Measure up 1 inch from the bottom corner on each of the side cutting lines and make dots at these points.

6. Using a curved ruler or drawing freehand, connect the dot made in Step 5 with each dot made in Step 6 to form a curved bottom cutting line, as shown.

7. To provide fullness for gathers, make three marks across the top cutting line to divide it into four equal segments.

8. Using the marks made in Step 7 as a guide, draw three slash lines to the bottom cutting line. They should be perpendicular to the top cutting line.

9. Cut out the pocket pattern along the cutting lines.

10. Slash into the slash lines up to but not through the bottom edge of the pattern.

11. Using another piece of paper, draw a vertical line to serve as a guide for centering the pocket pattern. Then center the pattern on the paper.

12. Fan out the pattern by spreading it about 1 to 2 inches apart at each of the slash lines—the sheerer the fabric you plan to use, the wider the spread should be.

13. Tape the pattern in place.

14. Connect the openings in the top edge with smooth lines.

15. Turn the center line into a grain line by drawing in arrow marks.

16. Trim around the pattern outline.

17. Lay the pocket fabric wrong side up on a flat surface. (To make two pockets, fold the fabric in half lengthwise, wrong sides out.)

18. Place the pocket pattern on the fabric, aligning the grain line of the pattern to the lengthwise grain of the fabric. Pin.

19. Cut along the pattern outline. Remove the pins and set the pattern aside.

20. To cut out the pocket band, draw a rectangle directly onto the fabric with dressmaker's pencil. Make its length the same as the pocket square (Step 1) and its width twice as wide as you want the finished band to be plus 1 inch for seam allowances. Be sure to draw the lines with the grains of the fabric.

21. Cut the band along the drawn lines. (If you are making two bands, pin the fabric layers together at the corners inside the rectangle before you cut.)

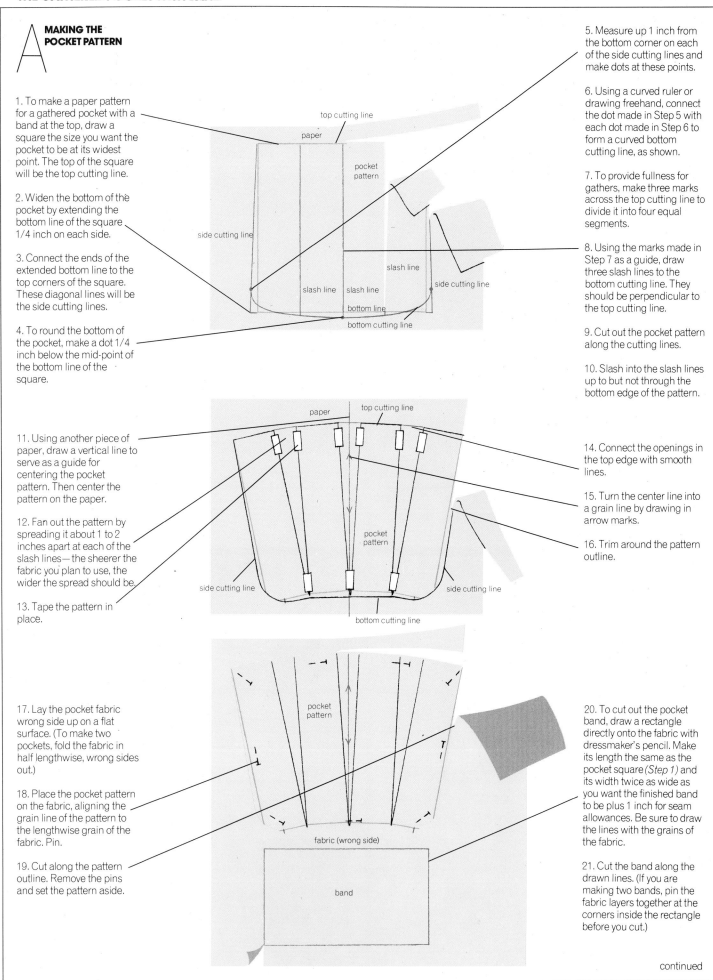

continued

B ATTACHING THE LINING TO THE POCKET

22. Cut out from lining fabric a pocket lining for each pocket, repeating Steps 17-19.

23. Trim off 1/8 inch from the side and bottom edges of the lining.

24. Pin together the pocket and lining, wrong sides out, at the top corners.

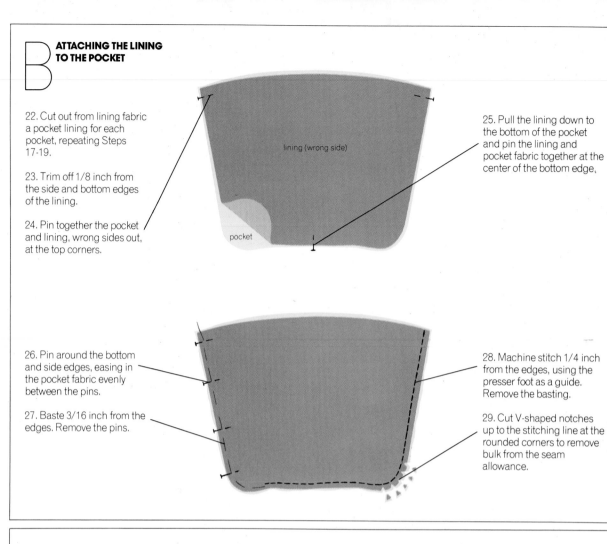

25. Pull the lining down to the bottom of the pocket and pin the lining and pocket fabric together at the center of the bottom edge,

26. Pin around the bottom and side edges, easing in the pocket fabric evenly between the pins.

27. Baste 3/16 inch from the edges. Remove the pins.

28. Machine stitch 1/4 inch from the edges, using the presser foot as a guide. Remove the basting.

29. Cut V-shaped notches up to the stitching line at the rounded corners to remove bulk from the seam allowance.

C GATHERING THE POCKET

30. Turn the lined pocket inside out by pushing the bottom up through the unstitched top edge.

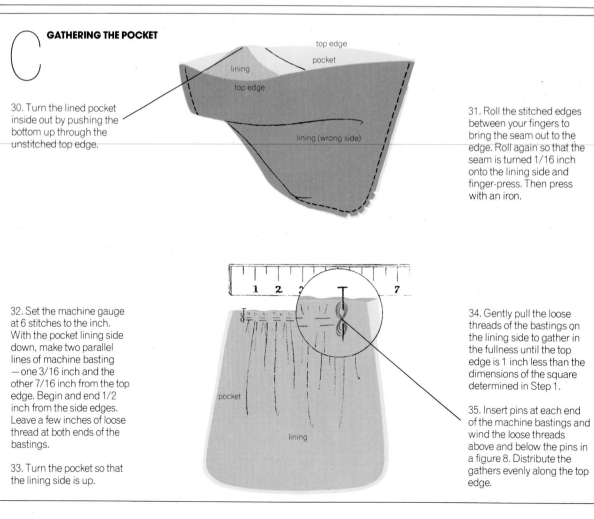

31. Roll the stitched edges between your fingers to bring the seam out to the edge. Roll again so that the seam is turned 1/16 inch onto the lining side and finger-press. Then press with an iron.

32. Set the machine gauge at 6 stitches to the inch. With the pocket lining side down, make two parallel lines of machine basting — one 3/16 inch and the other 7/16 inch from the top edge. Begin and end 1/2 inch from the side edges. Leave a few inches of loose thread at both ends of the bastings.

33. Turn the pocket so that the lining side is up.

34. Gently pull the loose threads of the bastings on the lining side to gather in the fullness until the top edge is 1 inch less than the dimensions of the square determined in Step 1.

35. Insert pins at each end of the machine bastings and wind the loose threads above and below the pins in a figure 8. Distribute the gathers evenly along the top edge.

D ⎵ MAKING AND ATTACHING THE BAND

36. Fold the band of the pocket in half lengthwise, wrong sides together, and press in the center crease.

37. Open out the band.

38. Cut a rectangle the same length and one-half the width of the band from an interfacing fabric.

39. Using dressmaker's pencil, draw a seam line 1/2 inch in from one long edge of the interfacing.

40. Position the interfacing on the band, aligning the unmarked edge with the center crease. Pin.

41. Baste the interfacing to the band inside the seam allowance of the marked edge. Remove the pins from the marked edge.

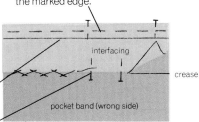

interfacing

crease

pocket band (wrong side)

42. Catch stitch (*Appendix*) the interfacing to the band along the center crease. Remove the remaining pins.

43. Turn the pocket so that the lining side is down.

44. Center the band on the pocket and align the interfaced edge with the top edge of the pocket. Pin.

45. Baste just above the drawn seam line. Remove the pins.

46. Reset the gauge at 10 to 12 stitches to the inch. Stitch on the seam line across the top edge. Remove the basting and the pins securing the gathers.

47. Trim the seam allowances to 1/4 inch.

48. Grade the seam (*Appendix*) by trimming the seam allowance of the interfacing as closely as possible to the stitching line.

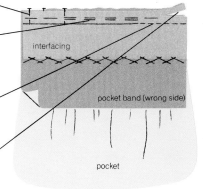

interfacing

pocket band (wrong side)

pocket

49. Turn the band away from the pocket along the top seam. Press the top seam, taking care not to flatten out the gathers.

50. To stitch the sides of the band, first fold down the band along the center crease, then fold up the 1/2-inch seam allowance on the edge of the band. Pin.

51. Machine stitch 1/2 inch from each side.

52. Trim the seams to 1/4 inch and cut the corners diagonally.

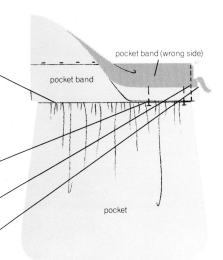

pocket band (wrong side)

pocket band

pocket

53. Turn the band inside out through the bottom opening with your fingers, and bring out the corners with a needle.

54. Place the pocket lining side up.

55. Fold under the 1/2-inch seam allowance on the bottom edge of the band, and press.

56. Slip stitch the band to the lining.

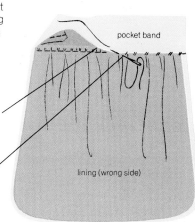

pocket band

lining (wrong side)

E ⎵ ATTACHING THE POCKET

57. Pin the pocket to the garment, making sure not to pull the sides out of shape or flatten the gathers.

58. Baste 1/8 inch from the side and bottom edges. Remove the pins.

59. Machine stitch close to the edges. Remove the basting. Press.

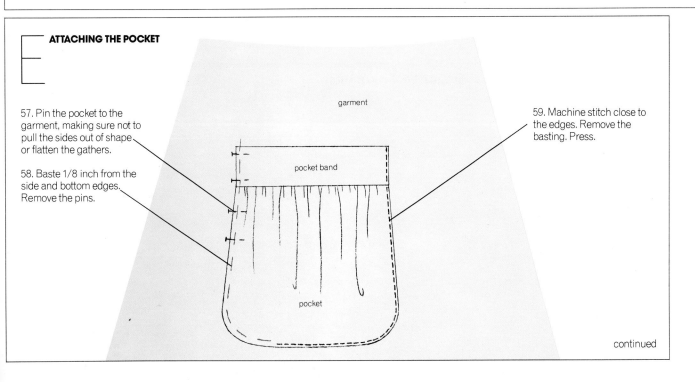

garment

pocket band

pocket

continued

Waistbands and trims for snug comfort

Stretchable edges—a collar, waistband and cuffs of rib knit, or an elasticized waistband—add comfortable give for long days of travel. The knit edgings come in step-saving, ready-to-attach tubelike pieces, or may be made from flat lengths of rib knit.

Rumpleproof sweater-knit finishes on critical parts of woven-fabric garments like the cropped jacket at right are easy to sew on (*opposite*). Fastening them to a knit-fabric garment, however, needs care, since the two knits may stretch differently. Patient pinning and stretching are required to avoid puckers. Applying an elasticized waistband (*pages 73-74*) draws on similar techniques of stretching and fitting.

THE OPEN RIBBED COLLAR ON A WOVEN-FABRIC GARMENT

A CUTTING THE COLLAR

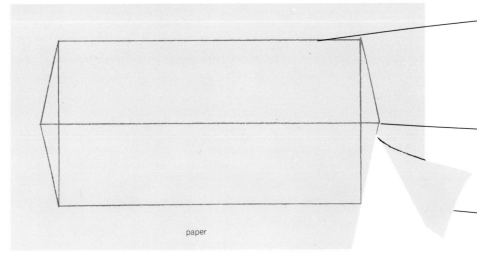

1. Assemble the garment following your pattern directions.

2. Determine the length of ribbing required by measuring around the garment neckline from center front to center front. Subtract 1 to 2 inches, depending on the stretchiness of the ribbing (*page 34*).

3. To make a paper pattern for the collar, draw a rectangle the length determined in Step 2 and twice the desired finished width of the collar.

4. For a collar with pointed corners at the front, first draw a line lengthwise through the center of the rectangle. Then extend the line 1 inch at both ends and draw lines from the corners of the rectangle to the ends of the center line.

5. Cut out the pattern.

paper

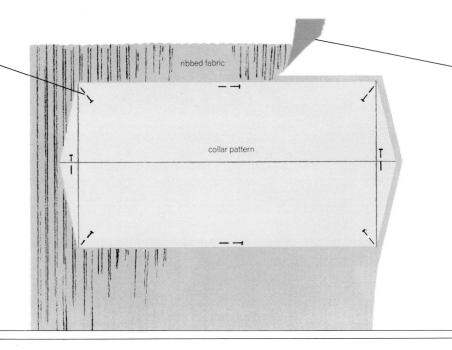

6. Pin the pattern to a piece of ribbed knit fabric with the long sides of the pattern at right angles to the ribs.

7. Cut out the collar 1/4 inch outside the edge of the pattern on all sides. Remove the pattern.

ribbed fabric

collar pattern

B PREPARING THE COLLAR

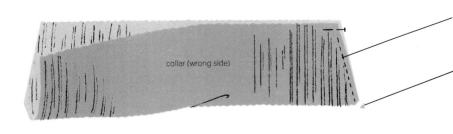

8. Fold the collar in half lengthwise, wrong sides out, and pin the ends together.

9. Machine stitch 1/4 inch inside the edges at each end, starting at the fold and ending 1/4 inch from the opposite side.

10. Clip the corners at the fold diagonally.

11. Turn the collar right side out. Pull out the corners with a pin.

collar (wrong side)

continued

C ATTACHING THE COLLAR

12. Machine stitch along the seam line of the garment to prevent the fabric from stretching as you work. Then clip the sharply curved portions of the neck seam allowances.

13. Spread out the garment, wrong side down.

14. Open the ribbed collar and pin one raw edge along the neckline of the garment 3/8 inch inside the garment edge. Stretching the ribbing slightly to fit it, pin it to the garment first at the center back and center front and then in between.

15. Baste the collar edge to the garment, removing the pins as you sew.

16. Machine stitch 1/4 inch inside the edge of the collar. Remove the basting.

17. Trim the garment seam allowance to 3/8 inch.

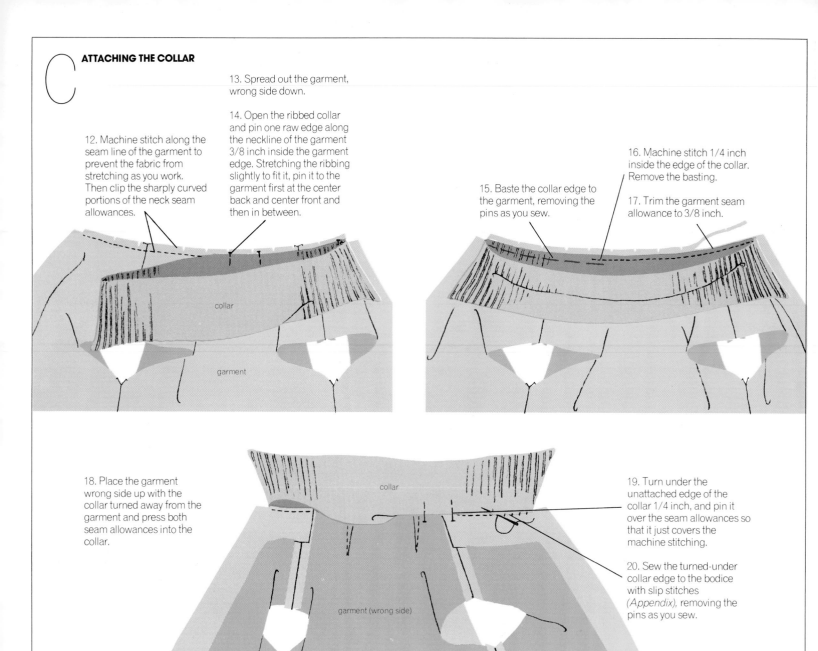

collar

garment

18. Place the garment wrong side up with the collar turned away from the garment and press both seam allowances into the collar.

19. Turn under the unattached edge of the collar 1/4 inch, and pin it over the seam allowances so that it just covers the machine stitching.

20. Sew the turned-under collar edge to the bodice with slip stitches (Appendix), removing the pins as you sew.

collar

garment (wrong side)

THE RIBBED WAISTBAND ON A WOVEN-FABRIC GARMENT

A CUTTING THE WAISTBAND

1. Assemble the garment bodice following your pattern directions.

2. Cut a rectangle of ribbed knit fabric for the waistband twice the desired finished height plus 1/2 inch and slightly longer than your waist measurement.

3. Fold the ribbing in half lengthwise and try it on around your waist, stretching the ribbing slightly until it fits comfortably. Mark the length with a pin.

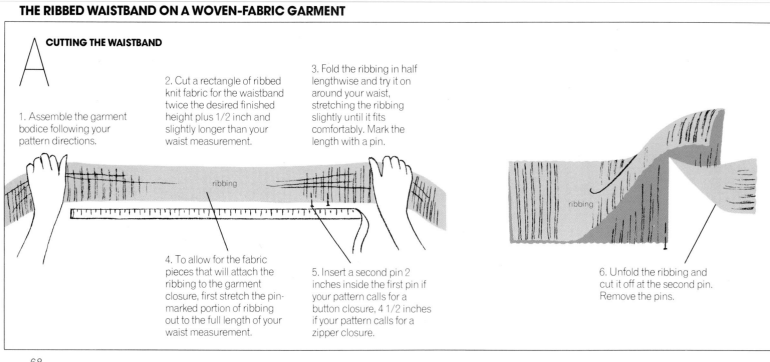

ribbing

4. To allow for the fabric pieces that will attach the ribbing to the garment closure, first stretch the pin-marked portion of ribbing out to the full length of your waist measurement.

5. Insert a second pin 2 inches inside the first pin if your pattern calls for a button closure, 4 1/2 inches if your pattern calls for a zipper closure.

ribbing

6. Unfold the ribbing and cut it off at the second pin. Remove the pins.

B ASSEMBLING THE WAISTBAND

7. To make the fabric end pieces that will attach the ribbing to the closure, cut two rectangles of garment fabric. Each rectangle should be 2 3/4 inches wide — measured on the crosswise grain of the fabric — and the same height as the unfolded ribbing.

8. With the wrong sides out, align the edges of the fabric pieces to the ends of the ribbing and pin.

9. Machine stitch the fabric to the ribbing 1/4 inch inside the edges. Remove the pins as you sew.

10. Press the seam allowances toward the fabric pieces.

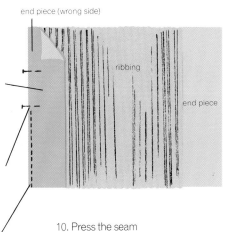

end piece (wrong side)

ribbing

end piece

11. Fold the waistband in half lengthwise, wrong sides out. Pin along each of the ends.

12. Machine stitch 1/4 inch inside each end, starting at the fold and ending 1/4 inch from the opposite side. Remove the pins as you sew.

13. Clip the corner of the seam allowances at the fold diagonally.

C ATTACHING THE WAISTBAND

14. Turn the assembled waistband right side out and pull out the corners with a pin.

15. Insert three pins along one raw edge of the waistband to divide the ribbed portion into four equal parts.

16. If your pattern requires it, gather the waist edge of the garment following the pattern directions.

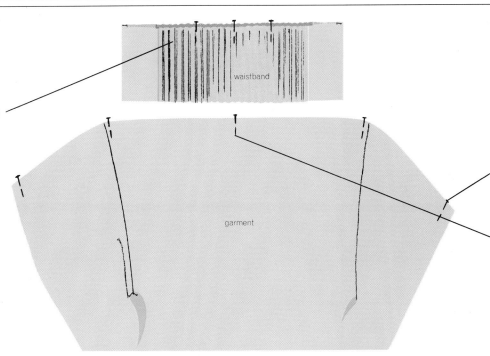

waistband

garment

17. Spread out the garment, wrong side down.

18. At each end of the garment edge, measure in 2 1/2 inches — the finished width of the fabric pieces on the waistband — and insert a pin.

19. Insert three more pins to divide the center section of the waist edge into four equal parts.

20. Open the waistband and place it over the waist edge of the garment so that the pin-marked edge of the waistband is 3/8 inch inside the pin-marked edge of the garment.

21. Match and pin the waistband and garment together at the pin markers and the front edges. Then pin in between the markers.

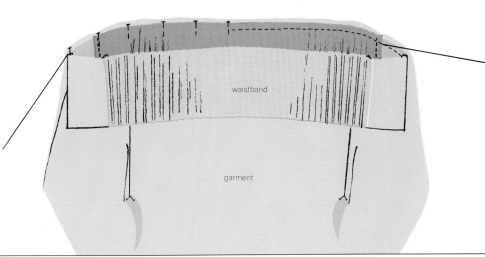

waistband

garment

22. Stretching the ribbing as you sew, machine stitch 1/4 inch in from the edge of the waistband. As you reach a pin, remove it.

23. Complete the waistband following the instructions in Box C, Steps 17-20, for the open ribbed collar on a woven-fabric garment (opposite).

THE RIBBED CUFF ON A WOVEN FABRIC GARMENT

A PREPARING THE CUFF

1. Cut a rectangle of ribbed knit fabric slightly longer than the circumference of your arm at the point where the cuff will go and twice the desired finished width of the cuff plus 1/2 inch.

2. Fold the ribbing in half lengthwise and try it around your arm, stretching it slightly until it fits comfortably. Mark the length with a pin.

3. Unfold the ribbing and trim it 1/2 inch beyond the pin. Remove the pin.

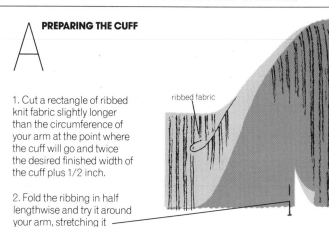

ribbed fabric

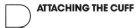

4. Fold the ribbing in half widthwise, wrong sides out, and pin the ends together.

5. Machine stitch the ends 1/4 inch inside the edges, removing the pins as you sew.

6. Press the seam open.

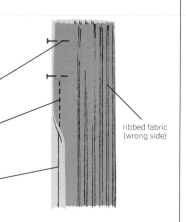

ribbed fabric (wrong side)

B ATTACHING THE CUFF

7. Following your pattern directions, close the underarm seam of the sleeve and—if necessary —gather the lower edge.

8. With the sleeve wrong side out, insert a pin into the lower edge at the seam. Then insert three more to divide the edge of the sleeve into four equal parts.

9. Turn the ribbed cuff right side out. Insert a pin into one raw edge at the seam; then insert three more pins to divide the raw edge of the cuff into four equal parts.

10. Slip the cuff inside the sleeve so the pin-marked edge of the cuff is 3/8 inch inside the sleeve edge.

11. Match the cuff seam with the sleeve seam, then match and pin the cuff and sleeve together at the pin markers.

12. Stretching the ribbing as you sew, machine stitch 1/4 inch inside the cuff edge. Remove each pin as you go

13. Trim the sleeve seam allowance to 3/8 inch.

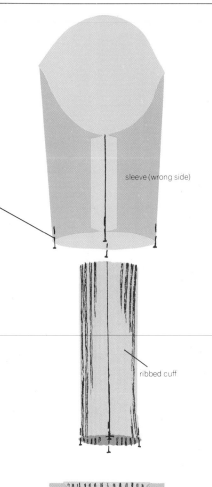

sleeve (wrong side)

ribbed cuff

ribbed cuff

C FINISHING THE CUFF

14. Bring the cuff out of the sleeve and press both of the seam allowances toward the cuff.

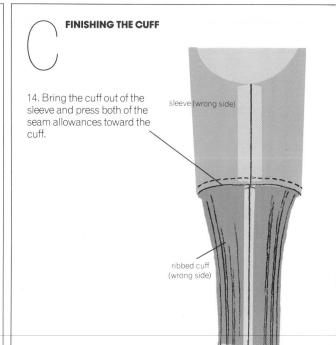

sleeve (wrong side)

ribbed cuff (wrong side)

15. Fold up the cuff. Turn under the unattached edge 1/4 inch and pin it over the seam allowances so that it just covers the machine stitching.

16. Sew the turned-under cuff edge to the sleeve with slip stitches (Appendix).

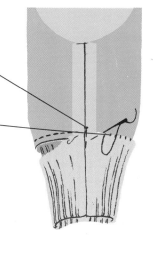

THE CONTINUOUS RIBBED OPENING ON A KNIT GARMENT

A PREPARING THE RIBBING

1. Assemble the garment, following your pattern directions.

2A. If you plan to use ribbing with a finished edge, cut a piece a few inches longer than your body measurement at the point where the ribbing will go.

2B. If you plan to use a double thickness of ribbed knit fabric, cut a rectangle a few inches longer than your body measurement at the point where the ribbing will go. For a turtleneck, make the rectangle four times the desired finished width of the ribbing plus 1/2 inch. For all other uses, make the rectangle twice the desired finished width plus 1/2 inch.

3. For a cuff or waistband, stretch the ribbing around your arm or waist until it fits comfortably. Mark the length with a pin. Be sure to fold the ribbing in half lengthwise if you will be using it in a double layer.

4. For a collar, measure your neck and mark the measurement on the ribbing with a pin. Then measure around your head and see if the pin-marked portion will stretch easily to that measurement. Adjust the length if needed.

6. Fold the ribbing in half widthwise, wrong sides out, and pin the ends together.

7. Machine stitch 1/4 inch inside the edges, removing the pins as you sew.

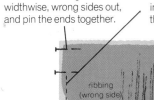

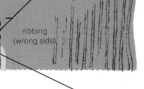

5. Trim the ribbing 1/2 inch beyond the pin.

8. Press the seam open.

B ATTACHING THE RIBBING

9. If you are using ribbed fabric, fold the ribbing in half, wrong sides together, and align the cut edges.

10. Insert a pin at the seam at the edge of the ribbing to be attached to the garment—the cut side of a doubled fabric, the unfinished edge of a finished band.

11. Insert three more pins along the same edge to divide the edge into four equal parts.

12A. For a crew neck or an armhole, measure from the seam line a distance equal to the desired finished width of the ribbing minus 1/4 inch; trim the garment edge at that point.

12B. If the ribbing is to project beyond the garment edge, trim the garment seam allowance to 1/4 inch.

13. Turn the garment wrong side out; insert a pin on the trimmed edge at the center back (at a garment seam for a cuff or waistband).

14. Insert three more pins to divide the trimmed edge into four equal parts.

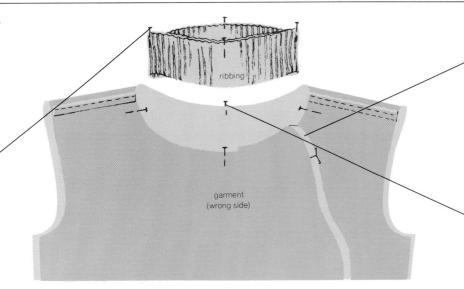

15. Slip the ribbing inside the garment opening and align the ribbing seam with the center back for a collar, the ribbing seam with a garment seam for a cuff or waistband.

16. Match and pin the raw edges of the ribbing and garment together at the pin markers.

17. Stretching both the ribbing and the garment fabric as you sew, stitch 1/4 inch inside the edges. Remove the pins as you go.

18. Turn the ribbing out of the garment opening and press the seam allowances toward the garment.

19. Turn the garment right side out.

20. Stretching all layers of fabric as you sew, run a line of machine stitching on the garment just below the ribbing. Catch the seam allowances in your stitches.

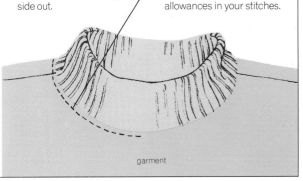

THE RIBBED MOCK TURTLENECK ON A KNIT GARMENT WITH A ZIPPER

A PREPARING THE COLLAR

1. Following your pattern directions, assemble the garment up to the point where you are ready to attach the collar.

2. Cut a rectangle of ribbed knit fabric slightly longer than your neck measurement and twice the desired width of the finished collar plus 1/2 inch.

3. Try the ribbing around your neck and adjust it until it fits snugly in a relaxed position. Mark the length with a pin. Be sure to fold the ribbing fabric in half lengthwise before you try it on.

4. Trim the ribbing to its final length at the pin.

5. Bring the ends of the ribbing next to each other so they just touch. Then join them with machine zigzag stitching. This is a temporary seam which will be removed when you put in the zipper.

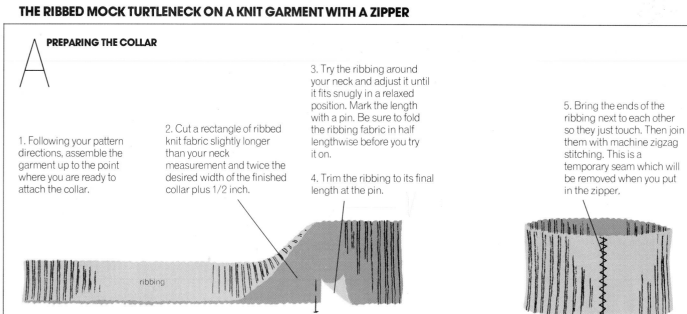

B ATTACHING THE COLLAR

6. Turn the collar right side out and insert a pin at the seam along one edge.

7. Insert three more pins along the same edge to divide the edge into four equal parts.

8. Turn the garment wrong side out and trim the seam allowances at the neck opening to 1/4 inch.

9. Insert one pin at the center back on the trimmed edge of the garment.

10. Insert three more pins to divide the neck edge into four equal parts.

11. Place the collar inside the neck opening and align the collar seam with the center back.

12. Match and pin the raw edges of the collar and garment together at the pin markers.

13. Stretching the ribbing and the garment fabric as you sew, machine stitch 1/4 inch inside the neck edge. As you reach each pin, remove it.

14. Insert the zipper and complete the collar following the instructions for the exposed zipper for double-layered ribbed collars, page 47.

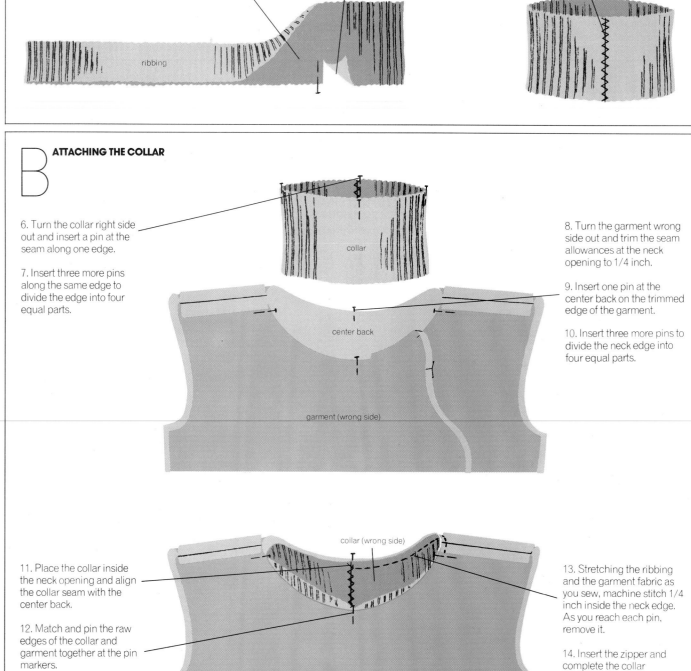

THE ELASTICIZED WAISTBAND ENCLOSED IN A CASING

1. Cut the garment sections following your pattern instructions, but make sure to provide a 1 1/4-inch allowance for the waistband casing. Then assemble the garment, stitching all seams closed up to the waistline edge. Press open the seams.

2. Turn the garment right side out.

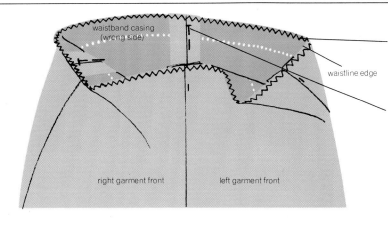

3. Sewing from the wrong side of the garment, finish the raw waistline edge with a line of machine zigzag stitches.

4. Insert a pin along the casing fold line at a seam. Pin from the wrong side of the garment. Then insert three additional pins along the fold line, dividing the waistline into four equal parts.

5. Cut a piece of 3/4-inch-wide elastic 1/2 inch longer than your waistline measurement.

6. Lap the ends of the elastic 1/2 inch and join them by machine stitching a small rectangle.

7. Insert a pin about 1 inch from the join. Then insert three more pins to divide the elastic into four equal parts.

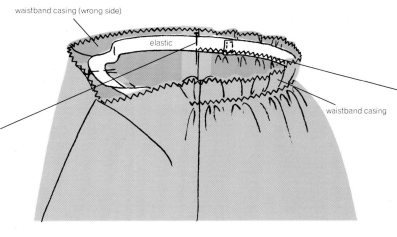

8. Place the elastic inside the garment, lining up the inner edge along the casing fold-line markings. Match and pin at the pin markers.

9. Stretching the elastic as you sew, attach the elastic to the garment by running a line of machine zigzag stitching just inside the inner edge of the elastic. As you reach a pin, remove it.

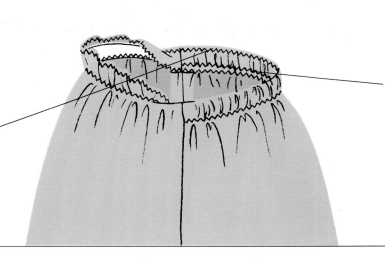

10. Fold the waistband casing to the inside of the garment along the inner edge of the elastic. Pin at the center front, center back and the sides.

11. Sewing from the wrong side of the garment and stretching the elasticized casing as you sew, run a line of machine zigzag stitching 1/4 inch from the unattached edge of the casing. Use the outer edge of the presser foot lined up with the edge of the casing as a guide. Remove each pin as you reach it.

THE ELASTICIZED WAISTBAND WITH MULTIPLE ROWS OF STITCHING FOR LIGHTWEIGHT KNITS

1. Cut the garment sections following your pattern instructions with the following exception: leave only a 1/4-inch seam allowance above the casing fold line or waist seam line. Then assemble the garment, stitching all seams closed up to the waistline edge. Press open the seams.

2. Turn the garment right side out.

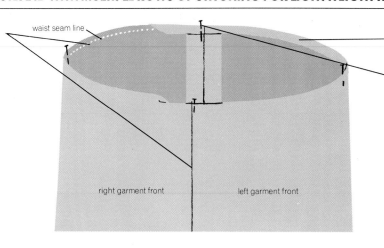

3. Fold the waistline edge of the garment to the wrong side 1/4 inch and press.

4. Insert a pin along the folded top edge of the garment at a seam. Pin from the wrong side of the garment. Then insert three additional pins along the folded edge, dividing the waistline into four equal parts.

5. Prepare a piece of 1/2- or 3/4-inch-wide elastic for the waistband as shown for the elasticized waistband enclosed in a casing (*page 73, Steps 5-7*).

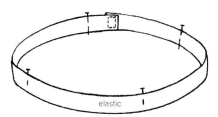

6. Place the elastic inside the garment, lining up the outer edge of the elastic just below the folded waistline edge of the garment. Match and pin at the pin markers, using one set of pins for pinning and removing the other set.

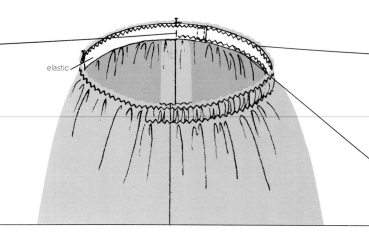

7. Sewing from the wrong side of the garment and stretching the elastic as you sew, run a line of machine zigzag stitching just inside the outer edge of the elastic. As you reach each pin, remove it.

8. Make a second line of zigzag stitching close to the inner edge of the elastic.

THE ELASTICIZED WAISTBAND WITH A HEADING FOR WOVEN GARMENTS

1. Cut the garment sections following your pattern instructions, but make sure to provide a 1 1/2-inch allowance for the waistband casing. Then assemble the garment, stitching all seams closed up to the waistline edge. Press open the seams.

2. Turn the garment right side out.

3. Fold the waistline edge of the garment to the wrong side 1/4 inch and press. Then fold along the casing fold line and press.

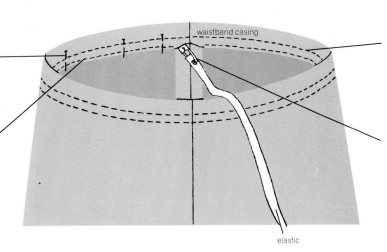

4. Pin the waistband casing to the garment, inserting the pins from the wrong side of the garment.

5. Sewing from the wrong side of the garment, machine stitch 1/8 inch from the inner edge of the casing. At the center back, leave an unstitched opening of about 1 1/2 inches for inserting the elastic. Remove the pins.

6. Make a second line of machine stitching 3/8 inch above the first one. Stitch completely around the garment without leaving an opening.

7. Cut a piece of 1/4-inch-wide elastic 1/2 inch longer than your waistline. Attach a safety pin to one end. Push that end of the elastic into the opening in the lower edge of the casing; thread the elastic through the casing.

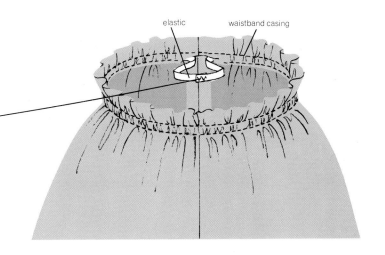

8. After the elastic has been pulled through the casing, remove the safety pin. Lap the ends by 1/2 inch and join them with a line of machine zigzag stitches. Stitch forward and then back for extra strength.

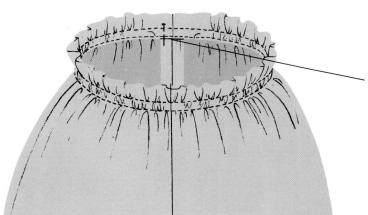

9. Pull on the waistband so that the ends of the elastic disappear into the casing.

10. Close the opening through which the elastic was inserted with machine stitching. Then adjust the fullness evenly around the waistline.

Seams to suit the fabric

Special care is necessary to ensure that the seams in crease-free knits and pseudo suedes lie flat. Double-faced pseudo suedes can be joined with lapped seams, as in this tunic, or with standard seams if the seam allowances can be bonded flat with fusible web *(opposite)*. With knits, a zigzag stitch lets the seam stretch (a straight stitch sewed with the fabric pulled taut will also work). Where needed, seam or bias tape helps stabilize the seams of springy knits.

THE LAPPED SEAM FOR DOUBLE-FACED PSEUDO SUEDE

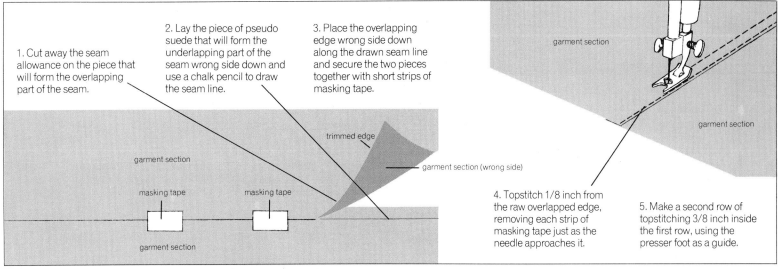

1. Cut away the seam allowance on the piece that will form the overlapping part of the seam.

2. Lay the piece of pseudo suede that will form the underlapping part of the seam wrong side down and use a chalk pencil to draw the seam line.

3. Place the overlapping edge wrong side down along the drawn seam line and secure the two pieces together with short strips of masking tape.

garment section

trimmed edge

garment section (wrong side)

garment section

garment section

masking tape

masking tape

garment section

4. Topstitch 1/8 inch from the raw overlapped edge, removing each strip of masking tape just as the needle approaches it.

5. Make a second row of topstitching 3/8 inch inside the first row, using the presser foot as a guide.

THE PLAIN SEAM FOR DOUBLE-FACED PSEUDO SUEDE

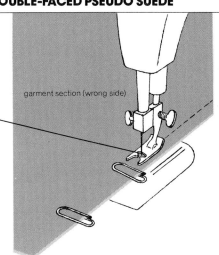

1. Place together, wrong sides out, the two pieces to be joined. Align the edges and secure the pieces with paper clips 4 inches apart.

2. Machine stitch 5/8 inch from the edges, using the stitching guide on the machine's throat plate to keep the seam straight. Remove each clip just as the needle approaches it.

garment section (wrong side)

3. Before flattening seam allowances with fusible web, test it on scrap fabric to see if it leaves marks or pulls apart when cool. Cut two strips of 1/2-inch-wide web the length of the seam.

4. Place one strip of web between the garment section and one seam allowance. Use a medium-hot iron and a pressing cloth to fuse the seam allowance flat.

5. Repeat Step 4 for the other seam allowance.

6. Brush up the fabric nap.

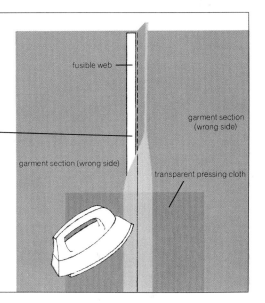

fusible web

garment section (wrong side)

garment section (wrong side)

transparent pressing cloth

THE DART FOR DOUBLE-FACED PSEUDO SUEDE

1. Make 1/4-inch clips at the ends of both side lines of the dart.

2. Slash the center line of the dart to within 1/8 inch of the point.

3. Fold the dart, aligning the clips. Pin in the seam allowance.

4. Machine stitch along the seam line, removing the pins as you go. Tie off the loose threads at both ends.

5. To flatten the dart, place 1/4-inch-wide strips of fusible web under the wide parts of the seam allowances of the dart, as shown in the plain seam for double-faced pseudo suede (above, Steps 3-6).

6. Center a 1-inch triangular piece of fusible interfacing over the point of the dart, placing the apex of the triangle on the dart seam, as shown. Press, using a tailor's ham.

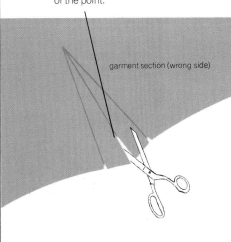

garment section (wrong side)

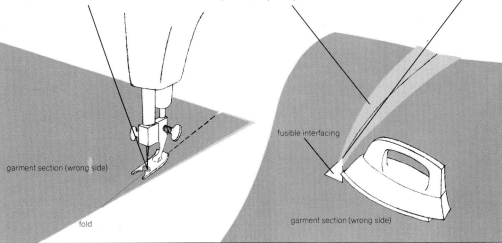

garment section (wrong side)

fold

fusible interfacing

garment section (wrong side)

THE BASIC STRETCH SEAM FOR KNITS

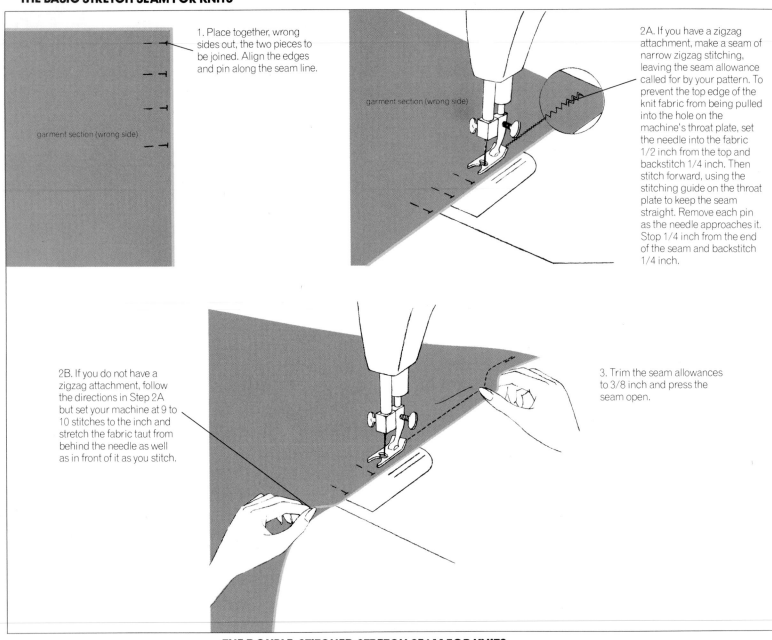

1. Place together, wrong sides out, the two pieces to be joined. Align the edges and pin along the seam line.

garment section (wrong side)

garment section (wrong side)

2A. If you have a zigzag attachment, make a seam of narrow zigzag stitching, leaving the seam allowance called for by your pattern. To prevent the top edge of the knit fabric from being pulled into the hole on the machine's throat plate, set the needle into the fabric 1/2 inch from the top and backstitch 1/4 inch. Then stitch forward, using the stitching guide on the throat plate to keep the seam straight. Remove each pin as the needle approaches it. Stop 1/4 inch from the end of the seam and backstitch 1/4 inch.

2B. If you do not have a zigzag attachment, follow the directions in Step 2A but set your machine at 9 to 10 stitches to the inch and stretch the fabric taut from behind the needle as well as in front of it as you stitch.

3. Trim the seam allowances to 3/8 inch and press the seam open.

THE DOUBLE-STITCHED STRETCH SEAM FOR KNITS

1. To prevent seam allowances on lightweight knits and sweater knits from curling and puckering the seam, join together the two pieces of fabric, as shown in the basic stretch seam for knits (above, Steps 1 and 2A or 2B).

2. Run a second line of stitching—either straight stitching, as shown here, or zigzag stitching—through both layers of the seam allowance 1/4 inch outside the first line of stitching. (Be sure to stretch the fabric taut if you are not using a zigzag stitch.)

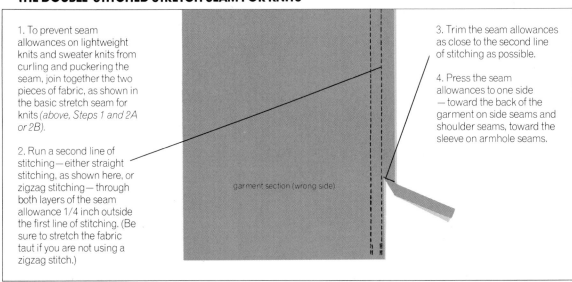

garment section (wrong side)

3. Trim the seam allowances as close to the second line of stitching as possible.

4. Press the seam allowances to one side —toward the back of the garment on side seams and shoulder seams, toward the sleeve on armhole seams.

THE STABILIZED SEAM FOR KNITS

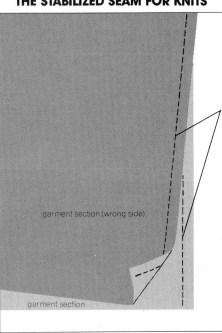

1. To keep a knit from stretching in an area of stress such as a shoulder seam, first run a line of machine stitching along the edge of each piece to be joined, leaving the seam allowance called for by your pattern. Start the stitching 1/4 inch from the top of the seam and end 1/4 inch from the bottom of the seam.

2. Place together, wrong sides out, the two pieces of fabric, matching the lines of machine stitching.

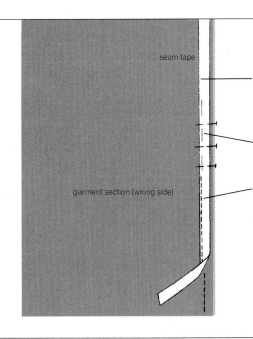

garment section (wrong side)

3. Cut a piece of preshrunk seam tape the length of the seam and place it over the seam allowance with one edge of the tape extending slightly beyond the stitched seam line.

4. Pin and baste the tape in place. Remove the pins.

5. Machine stitch the tape to the seam allowance, sewing through both pieces of fabric just inside the lines of stitching made in Step 1. Use the stitching guide on the machine's throat plate to keep the seam straight. Remove the basting.

6. Press the seam open.

THE SEMISTABILIZED SEAM FOR KNITS

1. To give knits a slight amount of flexibility in areas of moderate stress, such as at the hips, place together, wrong sides out, the two pieces of fabric to be joined. Align the edges.

2. Cut a piece of preshrunk bias tape the length of the seam. Then cut the tape in half lengthwise.

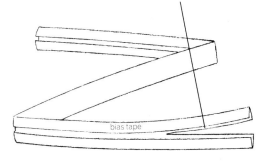

3. Open one half of the tape and place the fold line where the seam will be — that is, at a distance from the edge of the garment equal to the seam allowance called for by your pattern.

4. Pin and baste the tape in place. Remove the pins.

5. Machine stitch along the fold line of the tape. Remove the basting.

6. Press the seam open.

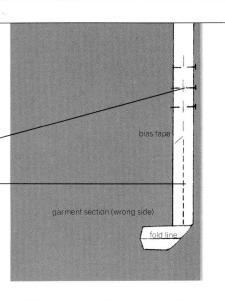

THE HAND-FELLED SEAM FOR SWEATER KNITS

1. Place together, wrong sides out, the two pieces of fabric to be joined, aligning the edges. Pin and baste the seam, then remove the pins.

2. Set your machine at 9 to 10 stitches to the inch and machine stitch, leaving the seam allowance called for by your pattern. Start 1/2 inch from the top of the seam and backstitch 1/4 inch. Then stitch forward, using the stitching guide on the throat plate to keep the seam straight. Stop 1/4 inch from the end and backstitch 1/4 inch. Do not stretch the fabric as you stitch. Remove the basting.

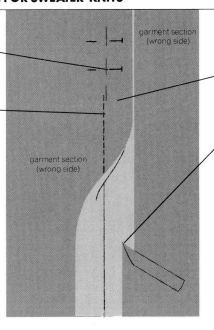

3. Press the seam allowances to one side — toward the back of the garment on side seams and shoulder seams, toward the sleeve on armhole seams.

4. Trim the underneath seam allowance to 3/8 inch.

5. Fold the wider seam allowance under the trimmed one. Then pin the seam allowances to the garment section.

6. Unravel a strand of yarn from leftover fabric. Using the yarn as thread, sew the folded edge of the seam allowance to the garment with a slip stitch (Appendix). Remove the pins.

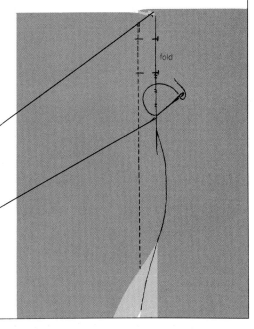

Easy finishes for hems and edges

For knitted and woven separates, the simplest finishes for edges and hems are often the most decorative —and for travel clothes they offer the added virtue of minimizing bulk. Several ingenious techniques can provide unusual touches such as an attractively rippling hem.

Topstitching creates its effects with nothing more than colored thread *(right)*. For highly visible top stitches, sew with a needle holding two threads. (If your machine has only one spool spindle, use two bobbins, one on top of the other.)

Other edgings include self-fabric bindings, which need only fabric scraps, and tape for reinforcing knits with a lot of give. And the lightest, easiest hem of all is the frilly lettuce hem designed for the stretchy fabrics so comfortable for travel.

SELF BINDING ON A CONTINUOUS OPENING FOR KNITS

A PREPARING THE BINDING

1. Assemble the garment, following your pattern directions.

2. Cut a strip of garment fabric 1 inch longer than the seam-line circumference of the opening and three and one half times the desired finished width of the binding. Cut the length on the crosswise grain of the fabric so the greatest stretch will be in that direction.

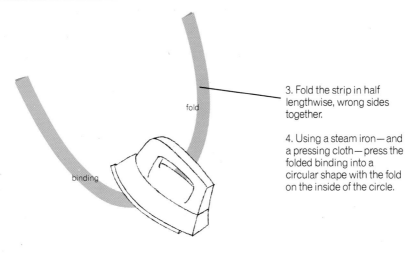

fold

binding

3. Fold the strip in half lengthwise, wrong sides together.

4. Using a steam iron—and a pressing cloth—press the folded binding into a circular shape with the fold on the inside of the circle.

B ATTACHING THE BINDING

5. Turn the garment right side out.

6. Measure in from the seam line of the opening the desired finished width of the binding and stay stitch *(Glossary)* around the opening at this distance.

7. Trim off the seam allowance just inside the seam line.

8. Unfold the binding and place one end, wrong side up, at a seam or at the center back on a neckline. Overlapping the center back or seam 1/4 inch, align the binding with the trimmed garment edge and pin.

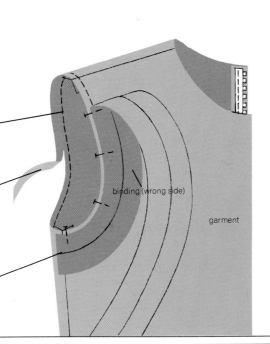

binding (wrong side)

garment

9. Pin around the opening, stretching the binding slightly, until you reach your starting point. Then cut off the excess binding, leaving another 1/4-inch overlap at the end.

10. Unpin the ends of the binding; stitch them together, making a 1/4-inch seam. Press the seam open.

11. Repin the joined ends of the binding to the garment.

12. Measure in from the edge of the opening the desired finished width of the binding; run a line of stitching parallel to the edge at this distance. Make sure this stitching line is just inside the stitching already on the garment. Remove the pins as you sew.

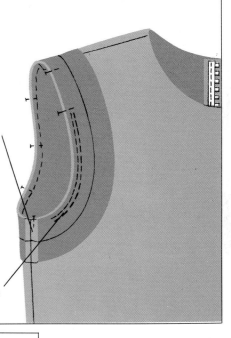

C FINISHING THE OPENING

13. Turn the binding up and over the seam allowances and baste it in place.

14. Press the binding.

15. Run a line of machine stitching close to the inner edge of the binding, sewing either on the garment, as shown, or on the binding. Remove the basting.

16. On the inside of the garment, trim the binding along the stitching made in the previous step.

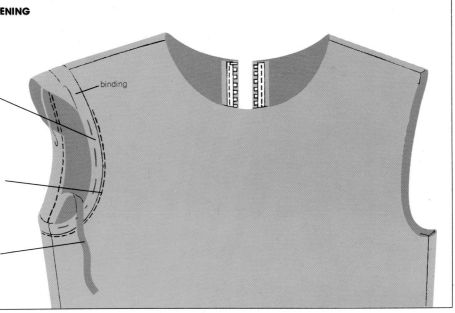

binding

SELF-BINDING ON A ZIPPERED NECKLINE FOR KNITS

A PREPARING THE GARMENT

1. Assemble the garment, following your pattern directions.

2. Turn the garment right side out. Measure in from the neck seam line the desired finished width of the binding and stay stitch (Glossary) around the neck at this distance.

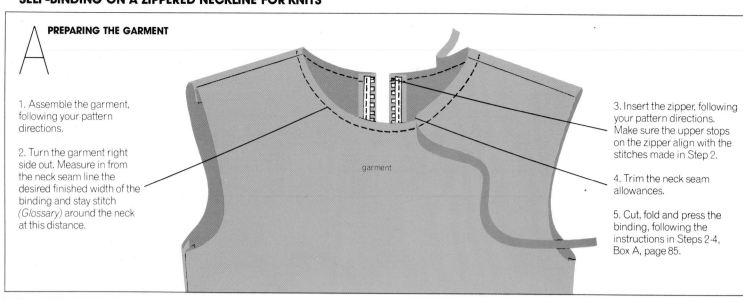

3. Insert the zipper, following your pattern directions. Make sure the upper stops on the zipper align with the stitches made in Step 2.

4. Trim the neck seam allowances.

5. Cut, fold and press the binding, following the instructions in Steps 2-4, Box A, page 85.

B ATTACHING THE BINDING

6. Unfold the binding.

7. With the garment right side out, place one binding end wrong side up at one side of the zipper, overlapping the opening 1/4 inch. Align the binding with the trimmed edge; pin.

8. Pin around the neckline, stretching the binding slightly, until you reach the other side of the zipper opening. Then cut off the excess binding, leaving another 1/4-inch overlap.

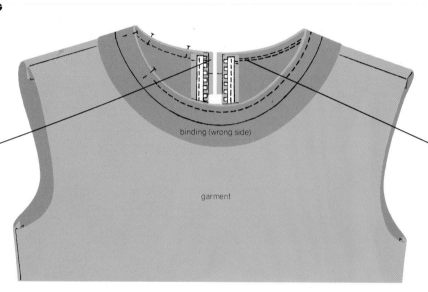

9. Measure in from the neck edge the desired finished width of the binding and run a line of machine stitching parallel to the edge at this distance. Make sure this stitching line is just inside the stitching already on the garment. Remove the pins as you sew.

10. If you want to flatten the binding to make it less prominent, press the seam open.

11. Turn up one end of the binding 1/4 inch. Then, starting at that end, turn the binding up and over the seam allowances, basting it in place as you proceed.

12. Turn up the other end 1/4 inch and finish basting.

13. Press the binding.

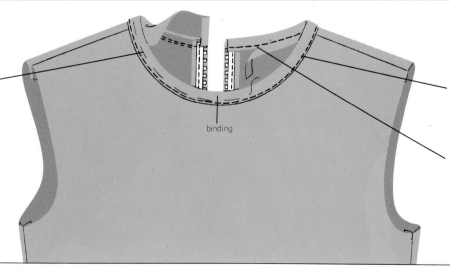

14. Run a line of machine stitching along the inner edge of the binding, as shown, or on the garment close to the binding. Remove the basting.

15. On the inside of the garment, trim the binding along the stitching made in the preceding step.

THE MOCK CUFF ON A SLEEVE

1. Check your pattern to see if the hem allowance is wide enough for a mock cuff. For a cuff with a narrow 1/8-inch tuck at the top, you will need 1 1/4 inches; for a wide 1/4-inch tuck, 1 1/2 inches. Lengthen the pattern if necessary.

2. Cut out the sleeve.

3. With the sleeve wrong side up, turn up the hem edge 1 inch and press.

4. Turn up the edge 1 inch again and press.

5. Depending on the size of the tuck you want, machine stitch either 1/8 or 1/4 inch inside the lower folded edge, stitching through all layers of fabric.

6. Turn the mock cuff down so it extends away from the rest of the sleeve. Complete the garment following your pattern directions.

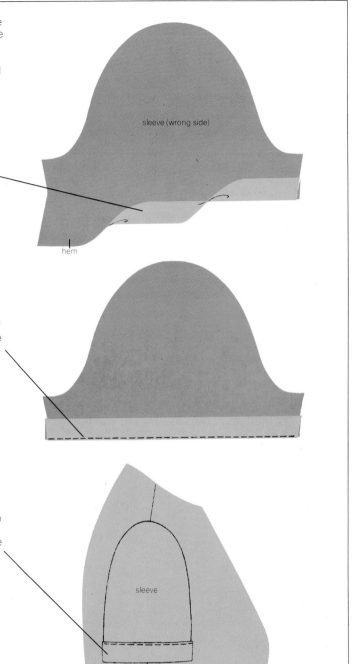

sleeve (wrong side)

hem

sleeve

THE LETTUCE HEM ON LIGHTWEIGHT KNITS

1. Assemble the garment following your pattern directions. Then try it on and mark the hemline.

2. Trim off the hem allowance 1/8 inch below the hemline.

3. Set your machine at 15 to 20 stitches to the inch. With the garment wrong side up, turn up the hem 1/8 inch; run a line of wide zigzag stitches along the hem edge, stretching the edge taut. Test on a scrap of garment fabric first.

4. As you complete the stitching the fabric will spring back and the wide zigzag stitches will become much narrower to give the hem edge a fluted frilly look like the edge of a lettuce leaf.

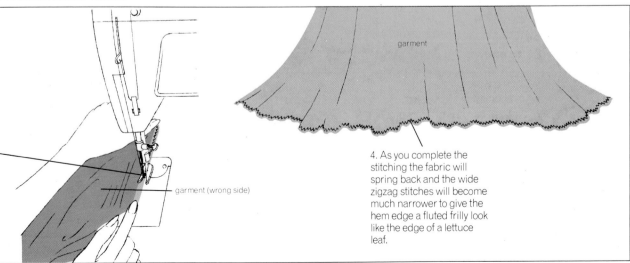

garment

garment (wrong side)

4
FASHIONS FOR THE FUN OF TRAVEL

ADJUSTING THE PATTERN FOR THE REVERSIBLE COAT

A TAKING YOUR MEASUREMENTS

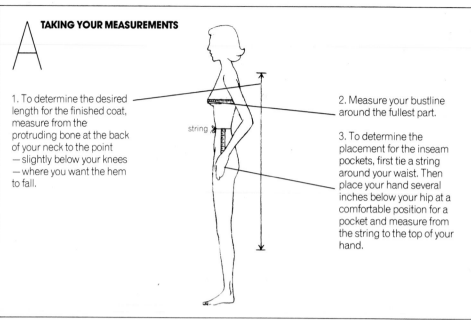

1. To determine the desired length for the finished coat, measure from the protruding bone at the back of your neck to the point —slightly below your knees —where you want the hem to fall.

string

2. Measure your bustline around the fullest part.

3. To determine the placement for the inseam pockets, first tie a string around your waist. Then place your hand several inches below your hip at a comfortable position for a pocket and measure from the string to the top of your hand.

B ADJUSTING THE LENGTH OF THE BACK PATTERN

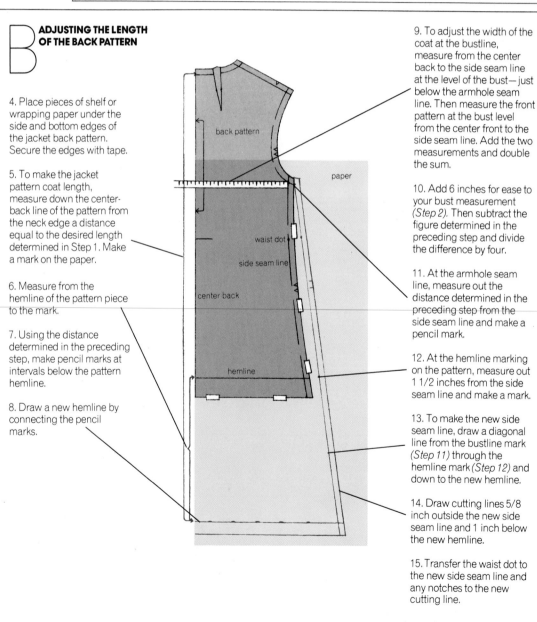

back pattern

paper

waist dot

side seam line

center back

hemline

4. Place pieces of shelf or wrapping paper under the side and bottom edges of the jacket back pattern. Secure the edges with tape.

5. To make the jacket pattern coat length, measure down the center-back line of the pattern from the neck edge a distance equal to the desired length determined in Step 1. Make a mark on the paper.

6. Measure from the hemline of the pattern piece to the mark.

7. Using the distance determined in the preceding step, make pencil marks at intervals below the pattern hemline.

8. Draw a new hemline by connecting the pencil marks.

9. To adjust the width of the coat at the bustline, measure from the center back to the side seam line at the level of the bust—just below the armhole seam line. Then measure the front pattern at the bust level from the center front to the side seam line. Add the two measurements and double the sum.

10. Add 6 inches for ease to your bust measurement (Step 2). Then subtract the figure determined in the preceding step and divide the difference by four.

11. At the armhole seam line, measure out the distance determined in the preceding step from the side seam line and make a pencil mark.

12. At the hemline marking on the pattern, measure out 1 1/2 inches from the side seam line and make a mark.

13. To make the new side seam line, draw a diagonal line from the bustline mark (Step 11) through the hemline mark (Step 12) and down to the new hemline.

14. Draw cutting lines 5/8 inch outside the new side seam line and 1 inch below the new hemline.

15. Transfer the waist dot to the new side seam line and any notches to the new cutting line.

C. ADDING THE INSEAM POCKET FLAP TO THE PATTERN

16. To add seam and cutting lines for the inseam pocket flap to the pattern, first mark the top of the pocket opening by measuring the distance determined in Step 3 down the side seam line from the waist dot.

17. To mark the bottom of the pocket opening, measure down the side seam line 6 1/2 inches from the top pocket marking.

18. To draw the pocket seam line, first draw a line 1 inch outside of and parallel to the side seam line at the pocket opening. Extend the line 1 1/2 inches above and below the pocket opening marks.

19. Draw a cutting line 5/8 inch outside the pocket seam line.

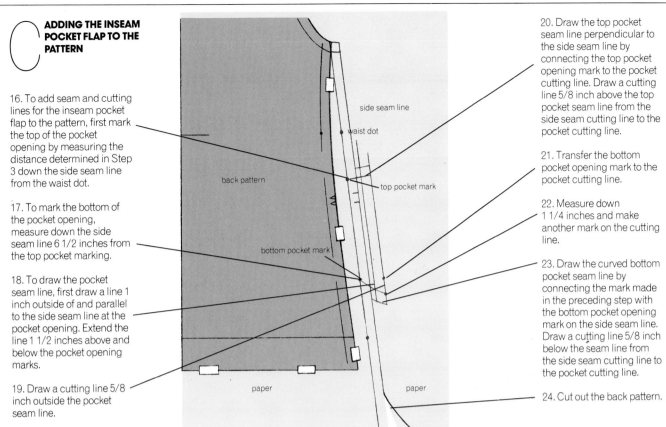

side seam line

waist dot

back pattern

top pocket mark

bottom pocket mark

paper   paper

20. Draw the top pocket seam line perpendicular to the side seam line by connecting the top pocket opening mark to the pocket cutting line. Draw a cutting line 5/8 inch above the top pocket seam line from the side seam cutting line to the pocket cutting line.

21. Transfer the bottom pocket opening mark to the pocket cutting line.

22. Measure down 1 1/4 inches and make another mark on the cutting line.

23. Draw the curved bottom pocket seam line by connecting the mark made in the preceding step with the bottom pocket opening mark on the side seam line. Draw a cutting line 5/8 inch below the seam line from the side seam cutting line to the pocket cutting line.

24. Cut out the back pattern.

D. ADJUSTING THE FRONT PATTERN

25. For a jacket front pattern with an all-in-one front facing, cut off the facing along the front fold line.

26. Tape pieces of shelf or wrapping paper underneath the side and bottom edges of the front pattern.

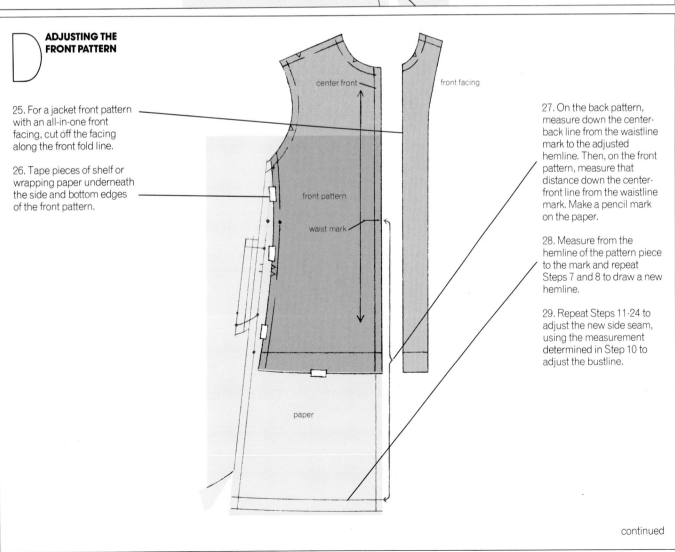

center front

front facing

front pattern

waist mark

paper

27. On the back pattern, measure down the center-back line from the waistline mark to the adjusted hemline. Then, on the front pattern, measure that distance down the center-front line from the waistline mark. Make a pencil mark on the paper.

28. Measure from the hemline of the pattern piece to the mark and repeat Steps 7 and 8 to draw a new hemline.

29. Repeat Steps 11-24 to adjust the new side seam, using the measurement determined in Step 10 to adjust the bustline.

continued

ADJUSTING THE SLEEVE PATTERN

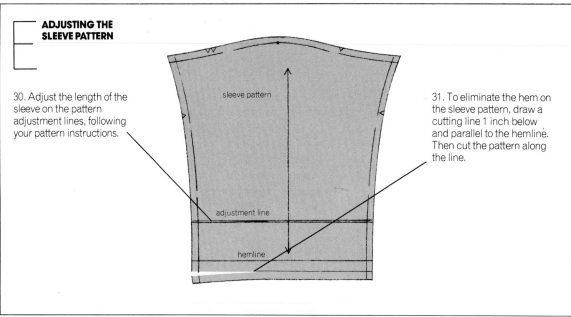

30. Adjust the length of the sleeve on the pattern adjustment lines, following your pattern instructions.

31. To eliminate the hem on the sleeve pattern, draw a cutting line 1 inch below and parallel to the hemline. Then cut the pattern along the line.

MAKING THE INSEAM POCKET PATTERN

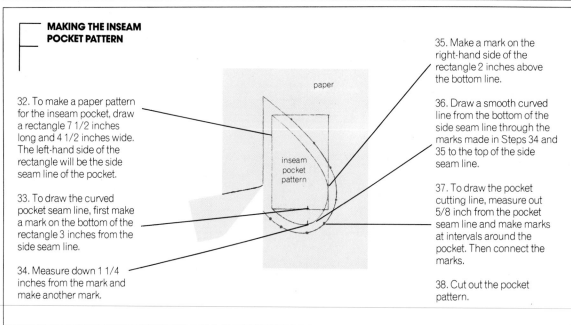

32. To make a paper pattern for the inseam pocket, draw a rectangle 7 1/2 inches long and 4 1/2 inches wide. The left-hand side of the rectangle will be the side seam line of the pocket.

33. To draw the curved pocket seam line, first make a mark on the bottom of the rectangle 3 inches from the side seam line.

34. Measure down 1 1/4 inches from the mark and make another mark.

35. Make a mark on the right-hand side of the rectangle 2 inches above the bottom line.

36. Draw a smooth curved line from the bottom of the side seam line through the marks made in Steps 34 and 35 to the top of the side seam line.

37. To draw the pocket cutting line, measure out 5/8 inch from the pocket seam line and make marks at intervals around the pocket. Then connect the marks.

38. Cut out the pocket pattern.

MAKING THE PATCH POCKET PATTERN

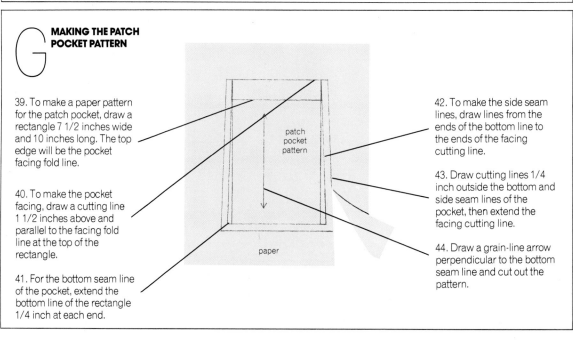

39. To make a paper pattern for the patch pocket, draw a rectangle 7 1/2 inches wide and 10 inches long. The top edge will be the pocket facing fold line.

40. To make the pocket facing, draw a cutting line 1 1/2 inches above and parallel to the facing fold line at the top of the rectangle.

41. For the bottom seam line of the pocket, extend the bottom line of the rectangle 1/4 inch at each end.

42. To make the side seam lines, draw lines from the ends of the bottom line to the ends of the facing cutting line.

43. Draw cutting lines 1/4 inch outside the bottom and side seam lines of the pocket, then extend the facing cutting line.

44. Draw a grain-line arrow perpendicular to the bottom seam line and cut out the pattern.

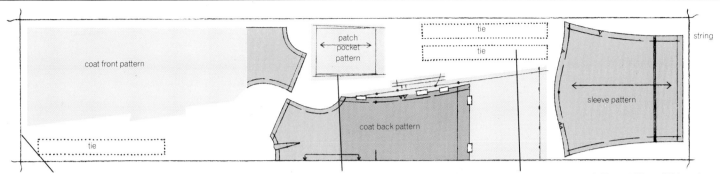

1. To decide how much fabric you need, use string to form a rectangle half the width of one of the fabrics you will use and several yards long.

2. Arrange the coat front, coat back, sleeve and patch pocket patterns inside the rectangle with the grain-line arrows parallel to the lengthwise strings. Do not use the inseam pocket pattern.

3. Adjust the length of the rectangle so that it just accommodates the pattern pieces, then measure it.

4. If both your coat fabrics are the same width, you will need the number of yards determined in Step 3 for each of them. If your coat fabrics are not the same width, repeat Steps 1-3 for the second fabric.

5. Fold the first coat fabric in half lengthwise with the selvage edges together and the wrong sides facing out. The first coat fabric will be padded, so do not use a water-repellent fabric for this layer.

6. Pin the pattern pieces to the fabric, following the layout determined in Step 2. If you plan to make a patch pocket on this layer of the coat, also pin the patch pocket pattern to the fabric.

7. Cut around the pattern pieces. Then, if the front ties will be made from this fabric, use the larger scraps of fabric to cut out six 16-by-2-inch front ties for the coat.

8. Use dressmaker's carbon and a tracing wheel to transfer the shoulder darts and the pocket opening markings to the wrong side of the fabric sections. Remove the pattern pieces.

9. Repeat Steps 5-7 to cut out the second coat fabric. Cut out the patch pocket and ties if you did not cut them from the first fabric.

10. Transfer all pattern markings to the wrong side of each fabric section with dressmaker's carbon and a tracing wheel, using the new lines where adjustments were made. Remove the pattern pieces.

11. To cut out the inseam pockets and patch pocket lining, place the lining fabric wrong side down; fold over one side 10 inches.

12. Fold down the facing on the patch pocket pattern.

13. Pin the two pocket patterns to the double fabric thickness, keeping the grain-line arrow of the patch pocket and the side seam line of the inseam pocket parallel to the fold.

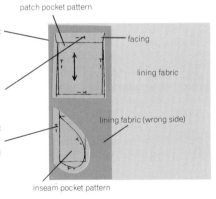

14. Cut around the pocket patterns. Then transfer the seam-line markings to the wrong side of the lining pieces with dressmaker's carbon and a tracing wheel. Remove the pattern pieces.

15. Fold the remaining lining fabric and cut out two more inseam pocket sections, following Steps 13 and 14.

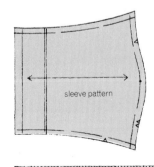
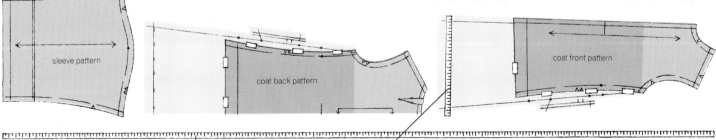
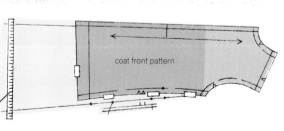

16. To determine how many yards of 18-inch-wide fusible web you will need to bond the batting to the second coat fabric, first arrange the coat front, coat back and sleeve pattern pieces in a row.

17. Measure from the top of the first piece to the bottom of the last piece.

18. Measure the width of the coat front pattern at the widest part. Then double that measurement and divide the result by 18. Round off any fraction to the next highest full number.

19. Multiply the figure determined in Step 17 by the figure determined in Step 18 to find the number of yards of fusible web you require.

ASSEMBLING THE REVERSIBLE COAT

A PADDING THE COAT

1. Stitch the shoulder darts on the coat back that you cut out of the first fabric. (Do not pad a waterproof fabric.) Then clip the darts and press them flat.

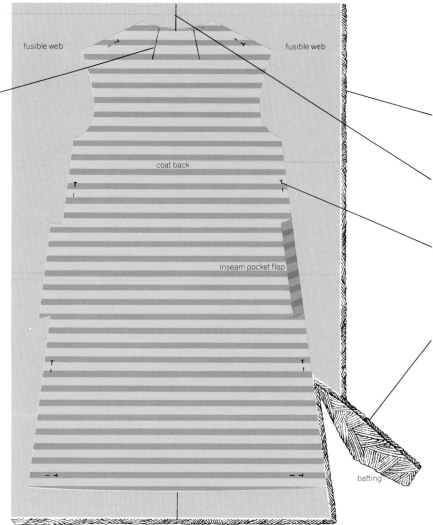

2. Lay the batting on a flat surface. If the full width is unmanageable, cut off a section that is at least 2 inches wider all around than the coat back.

3. Cover the batting with sheets of fusible web, butting the edges of the sheets.

4. Place the coat back, wrong side down, on top of the web and pin the layers of fabric, web and batting together.

5. Trim the batting to shape by cutting around the raw edges of the fabric. At the pocket opening, fold the flap back even with the side edge and cut out the batting along the fold.

6. To shape the batting at the shoulder darts, first remove any pins that are close to the darts. Make a clip into the neckline of the batting and web directly under the top of each dart, lifting the fabric out of the way as you do so.

7. Fold back the top edge of the fabric even with the bottoms of the darts. Then extend the cuts in the batting and web to the full length of each dart.

8. Using the cuts made in Step 7 as center lines, cut darts in the batting and web as wide as the fabric darts.

9. Butt the cut edges of the batting and web darts together and fold the top edge of fabric back into place. Insert a pin at each dart to keep it closed and hold the layers together.

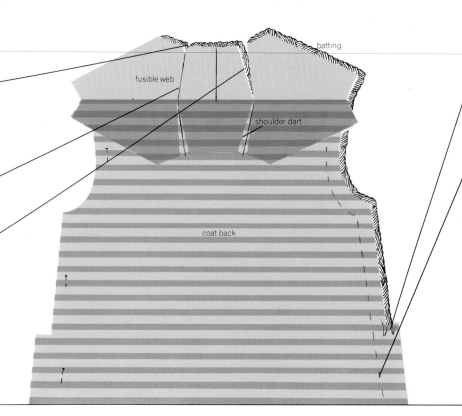

10. Make tailor tacks (*Appendix*) through all three layers at the top and bottom pocket opening marks on the side seam line and the pocket seam line.

11. Baste the three layers together 1 inch from the raw edges to prevent the batting from slipping. Remove the pins.

12. Fuse the fabric, web and batting together, following the instructions for the fusible web. Try out both the dry iron and steam iron methods on a sample of the three layers to determine which method works best for the fabric you are using.

13. Repeat Steps 2-12 to pad the coat front and sleeve sections that you cut out of the first fabric.

B FINISHING THE PADDED LAYER OF THE COAT

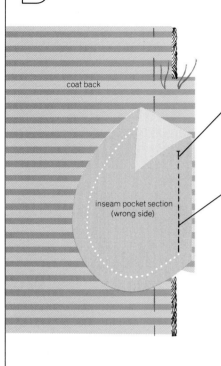

14. Place the padded coat back wrong side down; pin one inseam pocket section, wrong side up, to one pocket opening. Align the tailor tacks on the pocket opening seam line with the ends of the pocket side seam line. Pin another pocket section to the pocket opening on the other side of the coat back similarly.

15. Stitch along the pocket side seam lines, removing the pins as you go.

16. Place the padded coat front sections wrong side down; repeat Steps 14 and 15 to attach the other two pocket sections to the coat front pocket openings.

17. Press the seam allowances toward the pocket.

18. Pin the padded coat back and coat front sections together along the side seams, wrong sides out. Pin the pocket front and back sections together along the curved seam lines.

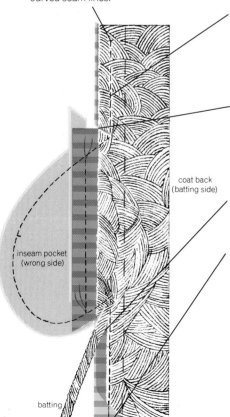

19. Machine stitch 5/8 inch from the raw edges; remove the pins as you go. Use the guide on the throat plate to keep the line of stitching straight. Start at the hem edge and stitch to the bottom pocket opening mark; pivot (Glossary) and stitch around the pocket to the top pocket opening mark. Pivot again; continue stitching up the side seam line to the armhole.

20. Clip the coat back seam allowances above and below the pockets.

21. Trim away the batting that extends beyond the seams, cutting just outside the stitching. Remove all bastings.

22. Press the seam allowances open above and below the clips made in Step 20.

23. Stitch the coat fronts and back together at the shoulder seams; insert the sleeves, following your pattern instructions. Use the throat plate guide to keep the line of stitching straight. Trim away the batting from the seam allowances; press them flat. Press the sleeve seam allowances toward the inside of the sleeve.

C MAKING THE PATCH POCKETS

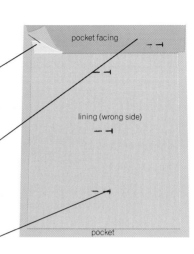

24. Trim off 1/8 inch from the sides and bottom edge of one pocket lining.

25. Fold down 1/2 inch at the top of the lining piece. Press.

26. Place one patch pocket wrong side down. Fold down the top of the pocket along the facing fold line. Press.

27. Center one lining section on top of one pocket section, wrong sides out. Slide the folded edge of the lining under the fold of the pocket and insert pins at the top and center of the sections.

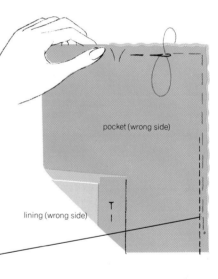

28. Turn the pocket over so the pocket fabric faces up. Baste along one side, easing the pocket fabric toward the center as you proceed to align the raw edge of the pocket fabric with the raw edge of the lining.

29. Continue basting around the bottom and the second side of the pocket, easing the fabric as you go.

30. Starting at the top fold, machine stitch 1/4 inch inside the raw edge around the sides and bottom of the pocket.

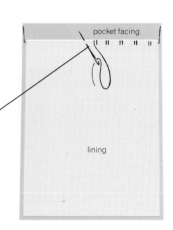

31. Turn the pocket right side out, pushing out the corners with the tip of a pair of scissors. Press, making sure the lining does not extend beyond the edges of the pocket.

32. Slip stitch the lining to the pocket at the top folded edge.

33. Repeat Steps 24-32 to assemble the other patch pocket.

continued

D ATTACHING THE PATCH POCKETS

34. Working on the garment sections that were cut out of the second fabric, stitch the shoulder darts, join the coat fronts to the coat back at the shoulder and side seams and insert the sleeves, following your pattern instructions.

35. Try on the coat and decide where you want to place the patch pockets.

36. Pin the pockets in place. Then baste and remove the pins.

37. Set your machine at 6 to 8 stitches to the inch and machine stitch the pockets to the coat front. To do this first bisect the top corner with a 5/8-inch-long diagonal line of machine stitching as shown. Then pivot (Glossary) and stitch around the pocket, pivoting at the corners. Bisect the other top corner with a diagonal line.

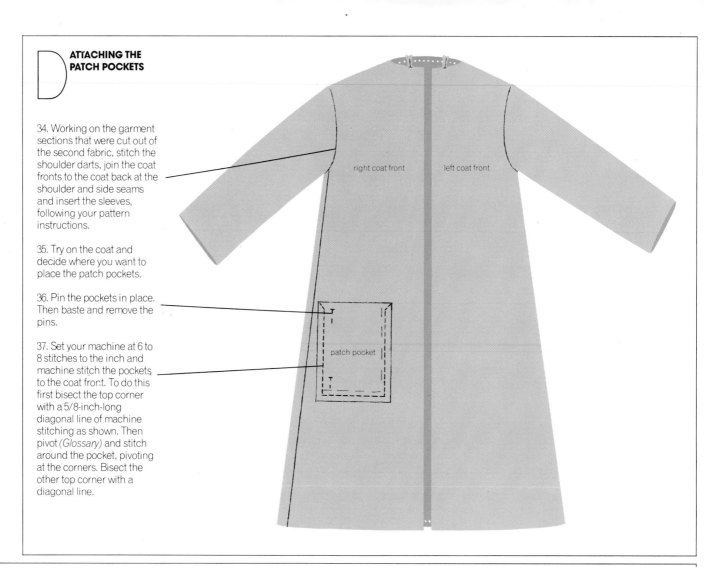

right coat front   left coat front

patch pocket

E ATTACHING THE TIES

38. Fold one tie in half lengthwise, wrong sides out.

39. Set your machine at 10 stitches to the inch and, starting at the fold, stitch across one end 1/4 inch from the edge. Then pivot and stitch down the side. Clip the corners diagonally up to, but not into, the machine stitching.

40. Repeat Steps 38 and 39 to make the other five ties.

41. Turn the ties right side out, pulling out the corners with a pin. Then press them flat.

42. Set your machine at 6 to 8 stitches to the inch and topstitch just inside the edges of each tie. Starting at the open end of each tie, stitch up one long side, across the short end, and down the other side —pivoting at the corners.

43. Pin the unstitched end of one tie to one of the unpadded coat fronts at the neck seam line. Align the raw edges of the tie with the raw edge of the coat front.

44. Pin a second tie to the neck seam line of the other coat front. Pin on the other ties 6 to 8 inches apart. Machine baste across each tie within the seam allowance. Remove the pins.

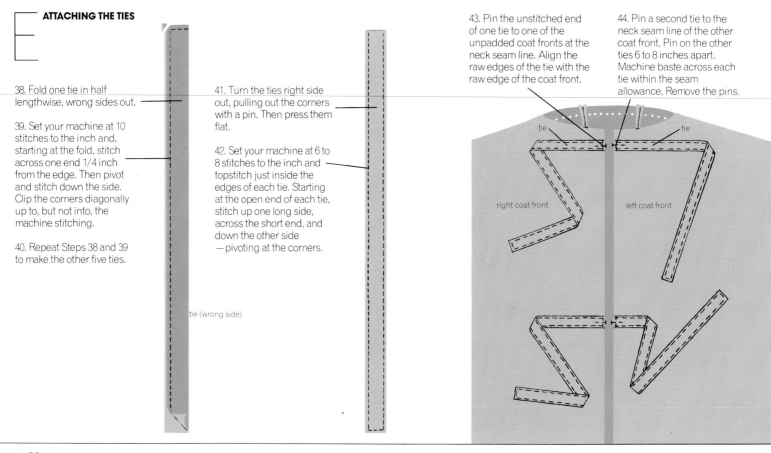

tie (wrong side)

tie   tie

right coat front   left coat front

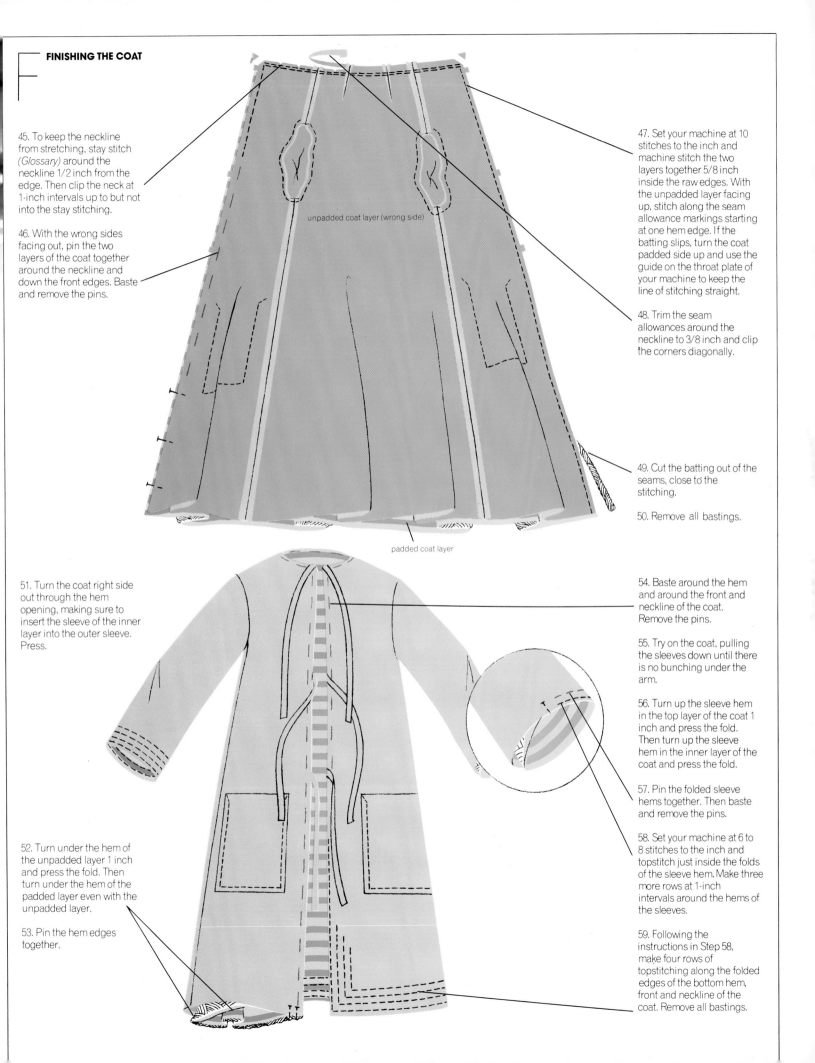

45. To keep the neckline from stretching, stay stitch (*Glossary*) around the neckline 1/2 inch from the edge. Then clip the neck at 1-inch intervals up to but not into the stay stitching.

46. With the wrong sides facing out, pin the two layers of the coat together around the neckline and down the front edges. Baste and remove the pins.

unpadded coat layer (wrong side)

padded coat layer

47. Set your machine at 10 stitches to the inch and machine stitch the two layers together 5/8 inch inside the raw edges. With the unpadded layer facing up, stitch along the seam allowance markings starting at one hem edge. If the batting slips, turn the coat padded side up and use the guide on the throat plate of your machine to keep the line of stitching straight.

48. Trim the seam allowances around the neckline to 3/8 inch and clip the corners diagonally.

49. Cut the batting out of the seams, close to the stitching.

50. Remove all bastings.

51. Turn the coat right side out through the hem opening, making sure to insert the sleeve of the inner layer into the outer sleeve. Press.

52. Turn under the hem of the unpadded layer 1 inch and press the fold. Then turn under the hem of the padded layer even with the unpadded layer.

53. Pin the hem edges together.

54. Baste around the hem and around the front and neckline of the coat. Remove the pins.

55. Try on the coat, pulling the sleeves down until there is no bunching under the arm.

56. Turn up the sleeve hem in the top layer of the coat 1 inch and press the fold. Then turn up the sleeve hem in the inner layer of the coat and press the fold.

57. Pin the folded sleeve hems together. Then baste and remove the pins.

58. Set your machine at 6 to 8 stitches to the inch and topstitch just inside the folds of the sleeve hem. Make three more rows at 1-inch intervals around the hems of the sleeves.

59. Following the instructions in Step 58, make four rows of topstitching along the folded edges of the bottom hem, front and neckline of the coat. Remove all bastings.

Five that mix and match

For traveling light, five easy-to-make pieces multiply into a wardrobe of costumes. At far left is a nylon jersey jacket and woven skirt and a scarf wrapped into a halter top—all in a book end-paper print. In the next picture, the same skirt is reversed to its solid-color side, and the top is a striped body suit that doubles as a playsuit *(see page 114).* At near left, the wrapped scarf of the first outfit, reversed to its striped side, tops a pair of knit pants.

Making the pants and sunsuit

The sunsuit at left, created from a maillot-style bathing suit pattern, owes much of its shapely appearance to the stretchy rib-knit fabric from which it is made. It also becomes a top for a pair of pants (*opposite*).

The bare-bones construction of the double-knit pants—achieved by eliminating the side seam and waistband from any pants pattern suitable for knits—enables them to hold their line through repeated packing and wearing. The scarf, which is seen on page 104 as a halter, reappears here wrapped into a turban and as a slinky neck fling. Yardages and cutting layouts will vary with the fabric used; to calculate both, see the instructions on page 119.

THE SUNSUIT

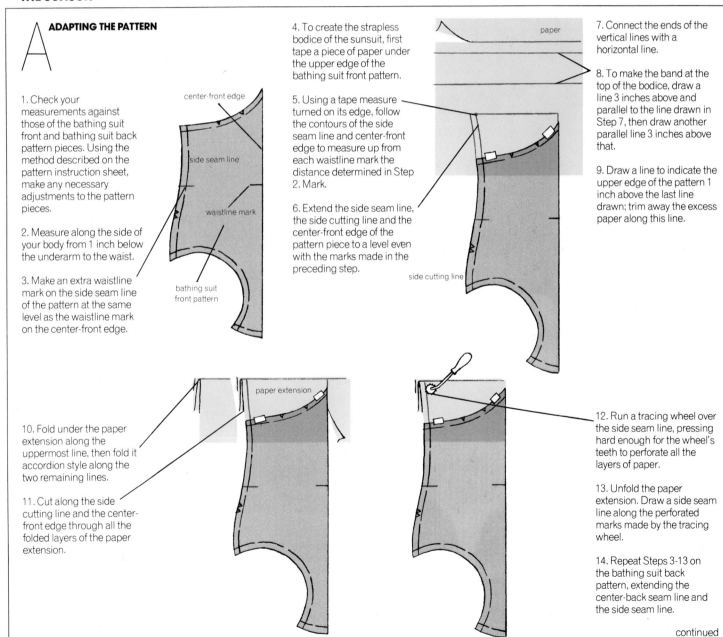

A ADAPTING THE PATTERN

1. Check your measurements against those of the bathing suit front and bathing suit back pattern pieces. Using the method described on the pattern instruction sheet, make any necessary adjustments to the pattern pieces.

2. Measure along the side of your body from 1 inch below the underarm to the waist.

3. Make an extra waistline mark on the side seam line of the pattern at the same level as the waistline mark on the center-front edge.

4. To create the strapless bodice of the sunsuit, first tape a piece of paper under the upper edge of the bathing suit front pattern.

5. Using a tape measure turned on its edge, follow the contours of the side seam line and center-front edge to measure up from each waistline mark the distance determined in Step 2. Mark.

6. Extend the side seam line, the side cutting line and the center-front edge of the pattern piece to a level even with the marks made in the preceding step.

7. Connect the ends of the vertical lines with a horizontal line.

8. To make the band at the top of the bodice, draw a line 3 inches above and parallel to the line drawn in Step 7, then draw another parallel line 3 inches above that.

9. Draw a line to indicate the upper edge of the pattern 1 inch above the last line drawn; trim away the excess paper along this line.

10. Fold under the paper extension along the uppermost line, then fold it accordion style along the two remaining lines.

11. Cut along the side cutting line and the center-front edge through all the folded layers of the paper extension.

12. Run a tracing wheel over the side seam line, pressing hard enough for the wheel's teeth to perforate all the layers of paper.

13. Unfold the paper extension. Draw a side seam line along the perforated marks made by the tracing wheel.

14. Repeat Steps 3-13 on the bathing suit back pattern, extending the center-back seam line and the side seam line.

continued

Labels in figure: center-front edge; side seam line; waistline mark; bathing suit front pattern; paper; side cutting line; paper extension

15. Follow the instructions on page 119 to determine how much fabric you will need, and how to lay out the pattern pieces.

16. Lay out and cut the knit fabric, then transfer all pattern markings to the fabric, including the lines drawn on the paper extensions in Box A.

17. Place the back sections together, wrong sides out, matching their raw, center-back edges. Pin.

18. Stitch the center-back seam, using the double-stitched stretch seam on page 78. Press the seam allowance to one side.

19. Place the front and back sections together, wrong sides out. Align the raw side edges on both sections. Pin.

22. Run basting stitches along the center line of tracing wheel markings.

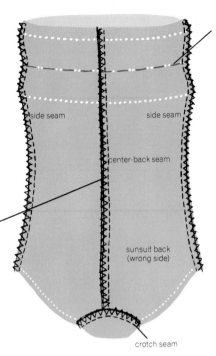

side seam
side seam
center-back seam
sunsuit back
(wrong side)
crotch seam

20. Stitch the side seams. Press the seams toward the back section.

21. Pin and stitch the crotch seam.

23. With the sunsuit wrong side out, fold down the top edge along the line of basting. Run a second line of basting close to the fold.

24. Turn under the raw bottom edge of the band 1/4 inch. Pin. Baste close to the fold and remove the pins.

25. Run a line of machine zigzag stitches along the bottom fold, leaving a 1-inch opening in the line of stitching into which elastic can be threaded.

26. To make a casing for the elastic in the bodice, run a second line of zigzag stitches 3/8 inch above the first. This time, however, stitch around the entire circumference of the garment.

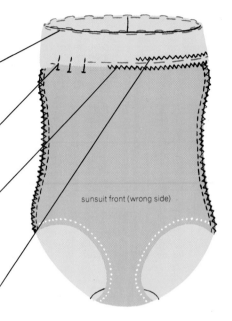

sunsuit front (wrong side)

27. To make a casing for the elastic at each leg opening, first turn up the raw edge of the leg opening 1/4 inch.

28. Turn up the folded edge 3/8 inch. Pin.

29. Baste close to the inner fold, stretching the fabric slightly as you baste. Remove the pins.

30. Run a line of machine zigzag stitches over the inner fold, leaving a 1-inch opening in the line of stitches. Remove all bastings from the garment.

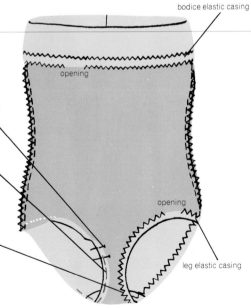

bodice elastic casing
opening
opening
leg elastic casing

31. Cut a length of 1/4-inch-wide elastic just long enough to wrap loosely around your bust, 1 inch below the underarms.

32. Attach a safety pin to one end of the elastic and thread it through the casing in the bodice. Pin the ends of the elastic together.

33. Cut two lengths of 1/4-inch-wide elastic just long enough to wrap loosely around the tops of your thighs.

34. Repeat Step 32 to insert the elastic into each leg opening.

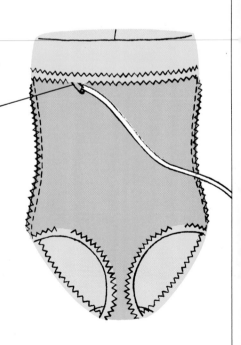

C) FINISHING THE SUNSUIT

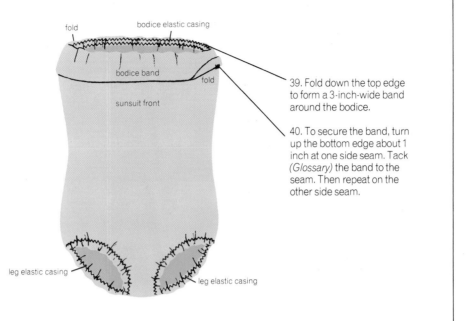

35. Turn the sunsuit right side out, and try it on. Tighten the elastic at the legs and bust until the suit fits comfortably. Repin.

36. Trim away the excess from each elastic, leaving 1/2 inch to overlap.

37. Overlap the ends of each elastic 1/2 inch and sew the ends together with several rows of zigzag stitches.

38. Close the opening in each of the casings with machine zigzag stitches.

39. Fold down the top edge to form a 3-inch-wide band around the bodice.

40. To secure the band, turn up the bottom edge about 1 inch at one side seam. Tack *(Glossary)* the band to the seam. Then repeat on the other side seam.

THE PANTS

A) ADAPTING THE PATTERN

1. Check your measurements against those of the pants front and pants back patterns. Using the method described on the pattern instruction sheet, make any necessary adjustments to the pattern pieces.

2. To eliminate the side seam from the pants pattern, overlap the pants front and pants back pattern pieces, matching the side seam lines from the hipline dot to the bottom of the leg. Tape the pattern pieces together.

3. Draw a new grain-line arrow parallel to the matched side seam lines. Cross out the original grain-line arrows.

4. To make a casing for the waistline elastic, first tape a piece of paper under the joined pattern pieces at their waistline edges.

5. Straighten the waist seam line by drawing a straight line from the center-front to the center-back edges. This drawn line will be the fold line for the waistline casing.

6. Draw a second line 1 1/4 inches above and parallel to the fold line. Trim off the excess paper above this line.

7. Fold under the paper extension along the line drawn in Step 5. Trim away the excess paper at the sides even with the center-front and center-back edges of the pattern pieces.

8. Cross out the waistline darts.

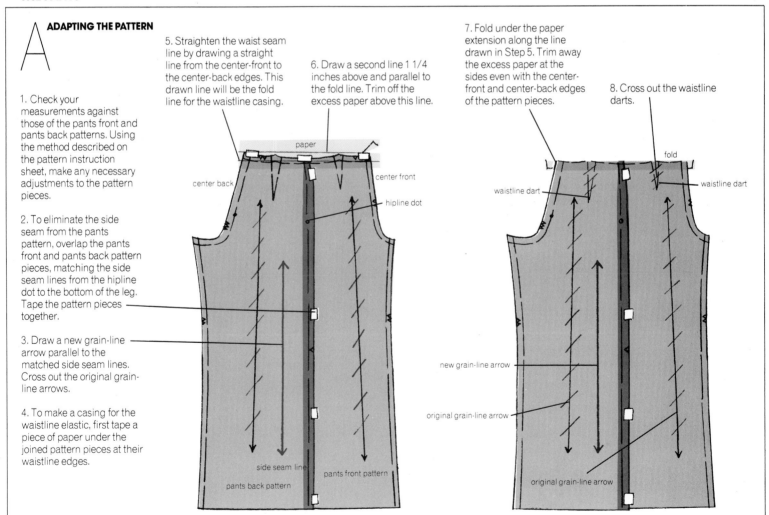

continued

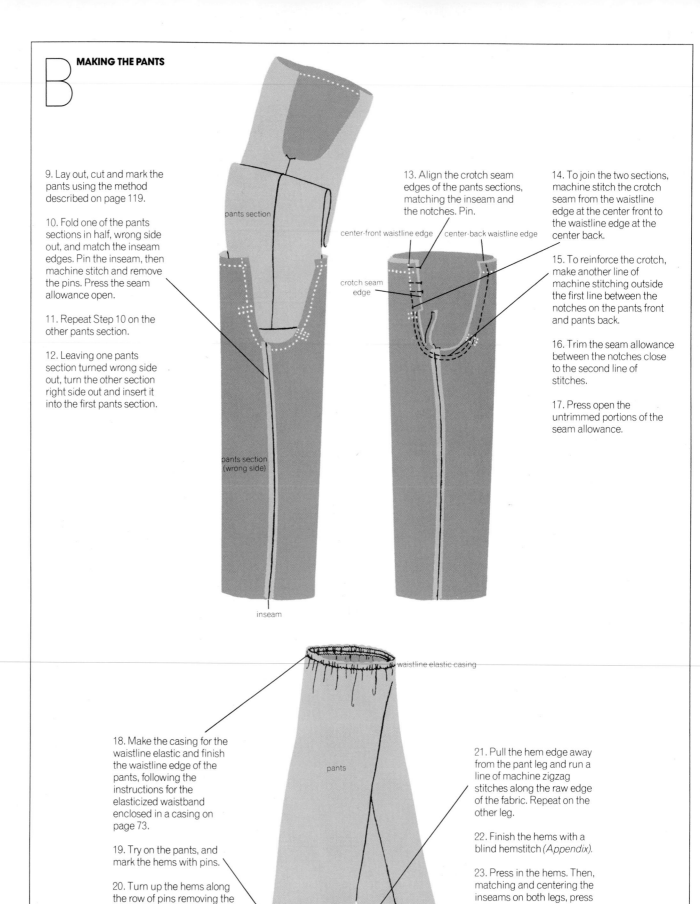

9. Lay out, cut and mark the pants using the method described on page 119.

10. Fold one of the pants sections in half, wrong side out, and match the inseam edges. Pin the inseam, then machine stitch and remove the pins. Press the seam allowance open.

11. Repeat Step 10 on the other pants section.

12. Leaving one pants section turned wrong side out, turn the other section right side out and insert it into the first pants section.

pants section

pants section (wrong side)

inseam

13. Align the crotch seam edges of the pants sections, matching the inseam and the notches. Pin.

center-front waistline edge   center-back waistline edge

crotch seam edge

14. To join the two sections, machine stitch the crotch seam from the waistline edge at the center front to the waistline edge at the center back.

15. To reinforce the crotch, make another line of machine stitching outside the first line between the notches on the pants front and pants back.

16. Trim the seam allowance between the notches close to the second line of stitches.

17. Press open the untrimmed portions of the seam allowance.

waistline elastic casing

18. Make the casing for the waistline elastic and finish the waistline edge of the pants, following the instructions for the elasticized waistband enclosed in a casing on page 73.

19. Try on the pants, and mark the hems with pins.

20. Turn up the hems along the row of pins removing the pins as you go. Baste near the hem folds.

pants

fold

21. Pull the hem edge away from the pant leg and run a line of machine zigzag stitches along the raw edge of the fabric. Repeat on the other leg.

22. Finish the hems with a blind hemstitch (Appendix).

23. Press in the hems. Then, matching and centering the inseams on both legs, press in the creases.

1. For patterns with pieces that are more than half the width of the fabric, knit or woven, and for knit fabrics with vertical ribs or horizontal stripes, skip to Step 9. For knit fabrics with a lengthwise center crease, skip to Step 17.

2. For all other fabrics and patterns, arrange string on a flat surface to form three sides of a rectangle representing the fabric. Make the width of the rectangle equal to half the width of the fabric and use several yards of string as a first approximation of length.

3. Arrange pattern pieces as efficiently as possible within the strings. Keep grain-line arrows parallel to the lengthwise strings and set pieces marked "place on fold" along one of the lengthwise strings.

4. To save fabric on most layouts, make a widthwise cut through the center of the scarf pattern so it is half the length of the finished scarf. Then use one pattern half for the string layout.

5. If you wish to bind the jacket with self-fabric, allow 1/2 yard extra on the layout for the bias binding.

6. Close off the open end of the string rectangle near the pattern pieces or just beyond the jacket binding allowance, and measure the length of the rectangle to get the amount of fabric you will need.

7. Use the same layout to arrange pattern pieces for cutting and marking.

8. Repeat Steps 2-7 for each woven or similar knit fabric you plan to use.

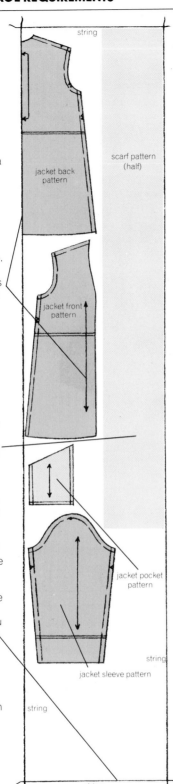

9. For all patterns with pieces that are more than half the width of knit or woven fabric and for vertically ribbed or horizontally striped knit fabrics, make a string rectangle the full width of the fabric and several yards long.

10. Make duplicate patterns (Appendix) for all pieces designed to be cut in duplicate or on the fold of the fabric.

11. Arrange the pattern pieces within the strings as efficiently as possible, keeping the grain-line arrows parallel to the lengthwise strings.

12. If you plan to use the fabric for the scarf, lay out the full pattern or cut the pattern in half widthwise and include both halves in the arrangement.

13. If you wish to bind the jacket with self-fabric, allow 1/2 yard extra on the layout for the bias binding.

14. Close off the open end of the string rectangle near the pattern pieces or just outside the jacket binding allowance, and measure the length of the rectangle to get the amount of fabric you will need.

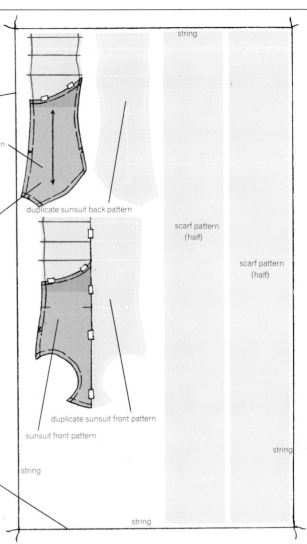

15. Use the same layout to arrange the pattern pieces for cutting and marking.

16. Repeat Steps 9-15 for each similar knit fabric you plan to use.

17. For knit fabrics with a permanent lengthwise crease, repeat Steps 2-8 if you plan to use a folded layout (page 35), but lay an additional string down the center of the rectangle to represent the center crease. If your pattern pieces are too wide for a folded layout, repeat Steps 9-16, laying a string down the center of the rectangle. Position the pieces between the strings or with the center string on an inconspicuous part of the pattern. Use the same layout to arrange the pattern on the fabric for cutting and marking.

Ribbed knit top and softly draped culottes

Pairing two slithery, form-fitting knitted fabrics—one ribbed, the other plain—turns this casual culotte-and-top outfit into a costume glamorous enough for evening wear. The easy-packing ribbed top is made by drafting a simple pattern from a series of rectangles. The companion culottes are adapted from a commercial pants pattern, shortened and flared. Both patterns are designed for very stretchy knits: a six-inch swatch of fabric should stretch to more than eight and a half inches.

FINISHING THE CULOTTES

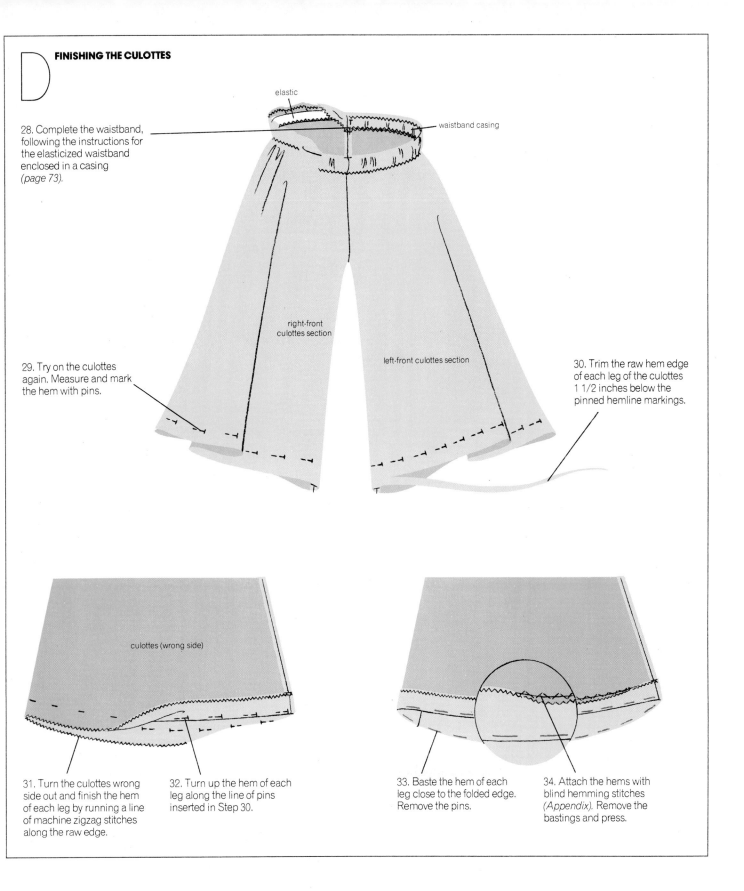

elastic

waistband casing

28. Complete the waistband, following the instructions for the elasticized waistband enclosed in a casing *(page 73)*.

right-front culottes section

left-front culottes section

29. Try on the culottes again. Measure and mark the hem with pins.

30. Trim the raw hem edge of each leg of the culottes 1 1/2 inches below the pinned hemline markings.

culottes (wrong side)

31. Turn the culottes wrong side out and finish the hem of each leg by running a line of machine zigzag stitches along the raw edge.

32. Turn up the hem of each leg along the line of pins inserted in Step 30.

33. Baste the hem of each leg close to the folded edge. Remove the pins.

34. Attach the hems with blind hemming stitches *(Appendix).* Remove the bastings and press.

A bare bikini and a cover-up

Made of two layers of nylon jersey —one striped, one plain—this bikini can be worn either side out. The bra is just an oblong, shaped and anchored by string, while the bottom is adapted from a purchased pattern. The djellaba cover-up, of crinkled mummy cloth with lettuce hems and roomy pockets, also does double duty as a bathrobe. It is made from a caftan pattern, slit down the front and given extra flare.

A ADJUSTING THE FRONT PATTERN

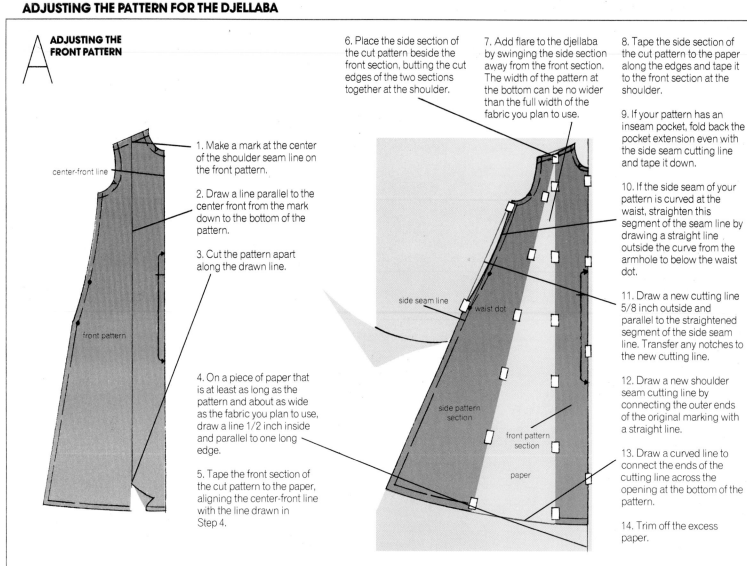

center-front line

front pattern

1. Make a mark at the center of the shoulder seam line on the front pattern.

2. Draw a line parallel to the center front from the mark down to the bottom of the pattern.

3. Cut the pattern apart along the drawn line.

4. On a piece of paper that is at least as long as the pattern and about as wide as the fabric you plan to use, draw a line 1/2 inch inside and parallel to one long edge.

5. Tape the front section of the cut pattern to the paper, aligning the center-front line with the line drawn in Step 4.

6. Place the side section of the cut pattern beside the front section, butting the cut edges of the two sections together at the shoulder.

7. Add flare to the djellaba by swinging the side section away from the front section. The width of the pattern at the bottom can be no wider than the full width of the fabric you plan to use.

8. Tape the side section of the cut pattern to the paper along the edges and tape it to the front section at the shoulder.

9. If your pattern has an inseam pocket, fold back the pocket extension even with the side seam cutting line and tape it down.

10. If the side seam of your pattern is curved at the waist, straighten this segment of the seam line by drawing a straight line outside the curve from the armhole to below the waist dot.

11. Draw a new cutting line 5/8 inch outside and parallel to the straightened segment of the side seam line. Transfer any notches to the new cutting line.

12. Draw a new shoulder seam cutting line by connecting the outer ends of the original marking with a straight line.

13. Draw a curved line to connect the ends of the cutting line across the opening at the bottom of the pattern.

14. Trim off the excess paper.

side seam line

waist dot

side pattern section

front pattern section

paper

B ADJUSTING THE BACK PATTERN

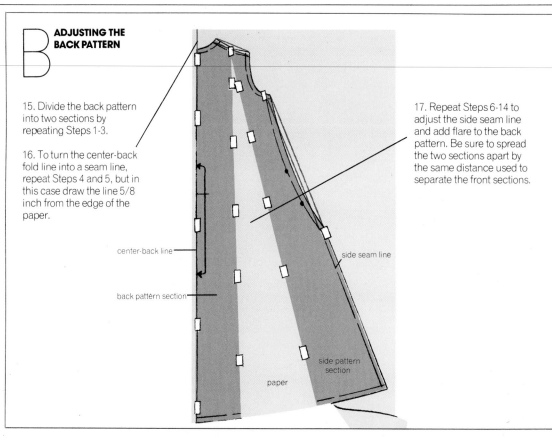

15. Divide the back pattern into two sections by repeating Steps 1-3.

16. To turn the center-back fold line into a seam line, repeat Steps 4 and 5, but in this case draw the line 5/8 inch from the edge of the paper.

17. Repeat Steps 6-14 to adjust the side seam line and add flare to the back pattern. Be sure to spread the two sections apart by the same distance used to separate the front sections.

center-back line

side seam line

back pattern section

side pattern section

paper

C | ADJUSTING THE SLEEVE PATTERN

18. Draw a line parallel to the grain-line arrow from the shoulder dot to the bottom of the sleeve pattern.

19. Cut the pattern apart along the drawn line, cutting up to but not through the top edge of the pattern.

20. Spread apart the cut edges of the pattern 4 to 6 inches at the hem.

21. Slide a piece of paper under the opening in the pattern and tape it in place.

22. Draw a curved line to connect the ends of the cutting line across the opening at the bottom of the pattern.

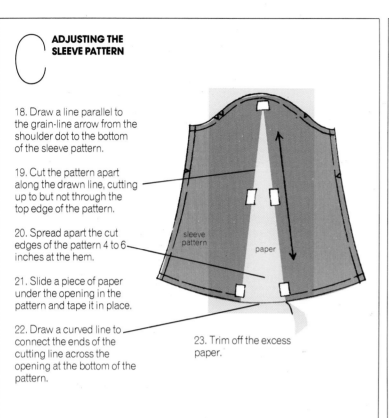

23. Trim off the excess paper.

D | ADJUSTING THE HOOD PATTERN

24. If your pattern calls for a lined hood, eliminate the lining to produce a lightweight hood by adding a 1/2-inch hem allowance to the front fold line of the hood pattern. To do this, use a piece of paper slightly longer than the pattern piece and draw a line on the paper 1/2 inch inside and parallel to one edge.

25. Tape the hood pattern to the paper, aligning the front fold line with the drawn line.

26. Trim off the excess paper.

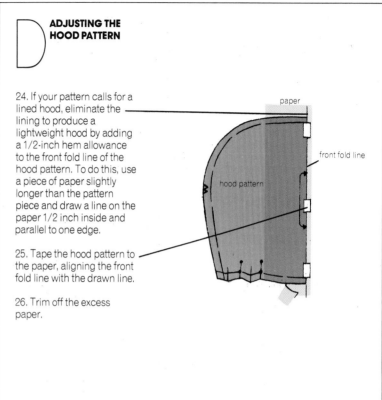

CUTTING AND MARKING THE DJELLABA

A | DETERMINING FABRIC REQUIREMENTS

1. To find how much fabric you need, arrange string on a flat surface to form three sides of a rectangle representing your fabric. Make the width equal to the fabric width; use several yards of string as an approximation of length.

2. Arrange the pattern pieces within the rectangle, following the suggested layouts overleaf.

3. Close the open end of the rectangle near the pattern pieces. Measure the length of the rectangle and multiply by two to provide for cutting the pattern out of a double thickness of fabric.

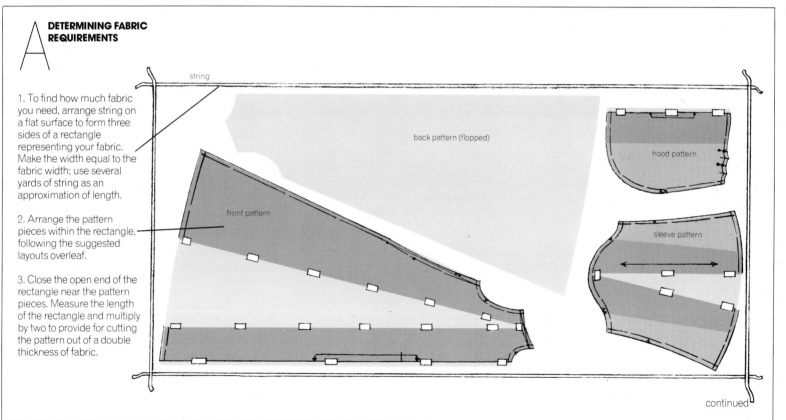

continued

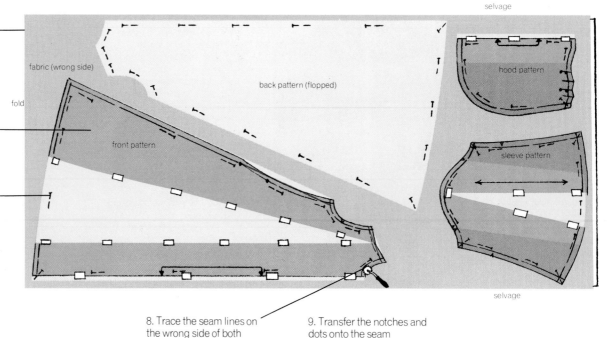

4. Fold the fabric in half widthwise, with the selvages together and the wrong sides facing out.

5. Arrange the djellaba front, back, sleeve and hood pieces on the double thickness of fabric as shown. Make sure that front and back fold lines and grain-line arrows are parallel to the selvages.

6. Pin the pattern pieces in place. Then cut them out.

7. Set aside a small scrap of fabric which includes part of a selvage for the button loop and two large scraps for the pockets.

8. Trace the seam lines on the wrong side of both fabric thicknesses with dressmaker's carbon and a tracing wheel.

9. Transfer the notches and dots onto the seam allowances of the fabric.

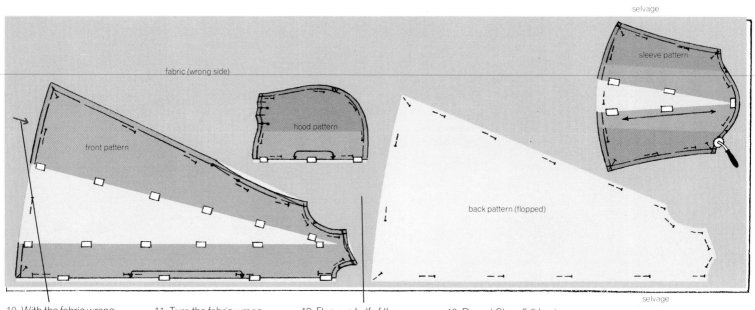

10. With the fabric wrong side up, mark the direction of the nap or design with arrows near both ends of the fabric.

11. Turn the fabric wrong side down and cut it in half widthwise.

12. Flop one half of the fabric wrong side up and place it on top of the other half so that the selvages align and the arrows point in the same direction.

13. Repeat Steps 5-9 to pin, cut and mark the fabric pieces.

MAKING THE DJELLABA

A ASSEMBLING THE DJELLABA

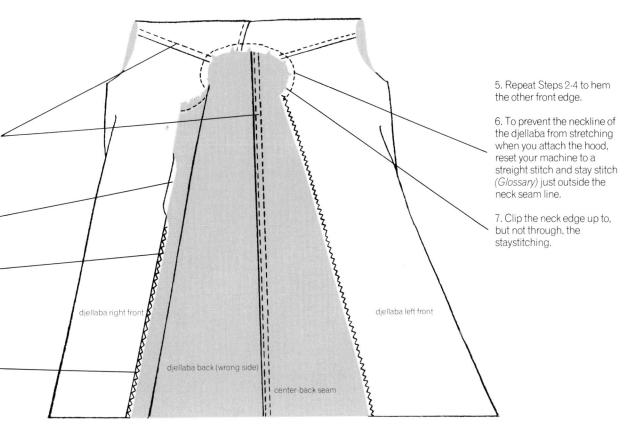

1. Using a flat felled seam (*Appendix*), stitch the djellaba back sections together at the center back. Then stitch the djellaba front sections to the back sections at the shoulder and side seam lines.

2. With the djellaba wrong side out, hem one front edge by first turning up the fabric 1/4 inch along the edge. Press.

3. Turn up another 1/4 inch to conceal the raw fabric edge and press again.

4. Turn the djellaba right side out and machine stitch along the folded double hem, using contrasting thread and a wide zigzag setting. The tips of the zigzag stitches should touch the front edge of the djellaba.

5. Repeat Steps 2-4 to hem the other front edge.

6. To prevent the neckline of the djellaba from stretching when you attach the hood, reset your machine to a straight stitch and stay stitch (*Glossary*) just outside the neck seam line.

7. Clip the neck edge up to, but not through, the staystitching.

djellaba right front

djellaba left front

djellaba back (wrong side)

center-back seam

8. Stitch the hood sections together along the center-back seam line with a flat felled seam. Make sure to turn the seam allowances in the direction of those on the center-back seam of the djellaba.

9. Repeat Steps 2-4 to hem the front edge of the hood.

10. Pin the pleats closed on the back of the hood, following your pattern instructions. Then machine baste across the pleats just outside the seam line and remove the pins.

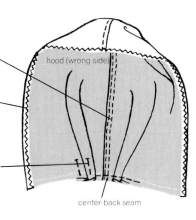

hood (wrong side)

center-back seam

11. Stitch the hood to the djellaba, following your pattern instructions.

12. To finish the neckline with a flat felled seam, first trim the garment seam allowance to 1/8 inch and the hood seam allowance to 3/8 inch. Then turn the hood seam allowance under in the usual manner and baste the seam to hold it flat around the curved neckline. Finally, machine stitch and remove the basting.

13. Insert the sleeves, following your pattern instructions. Then make a flat felled seam around the armhole, trimming the garment seam allowance to 1/8 inch and the sleeve seam allowance to 3/8 inch. Baste the sleeve seams before stitching.

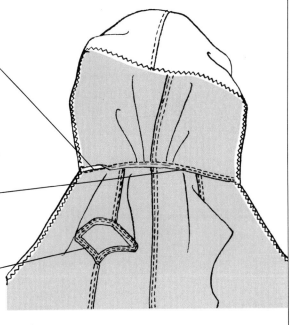

continued

B MAKING THE BUTTON LOOP

14. To make the narrow tube that will form the button loop, first fold the small scrap of garment fabric diagonally, bringing one segment of the selvage at a right angle to the other.

15. Press, then cut along the fold.

16. Draw a chalk line at least 6 inches long 1 inch inside and parallel to the cut edge.

17. Cut out the strip and cut off the ends of the strip at right angles to the sides.

18. Fold the strip in half lengthwise, wrong sides out. Pin.

19. Machine stitch from the cut edges at one corner end of the strip and stitch on a diagonal to 1/8 inch from the folded edge. Continue stitching 1/8 inch from the fold to the other end of the strip.

20. To turn the narrow tube right side out, cut a piece of thread 18 inches long. Double the thread and insert the loop through a thick tapestry needle. Knot the four thread ends together.

21. Take two stitches at the end of the tube close to where the stitching curves out to the end.

22. Insert the eye of the needle into the tube and work it through to the other end.

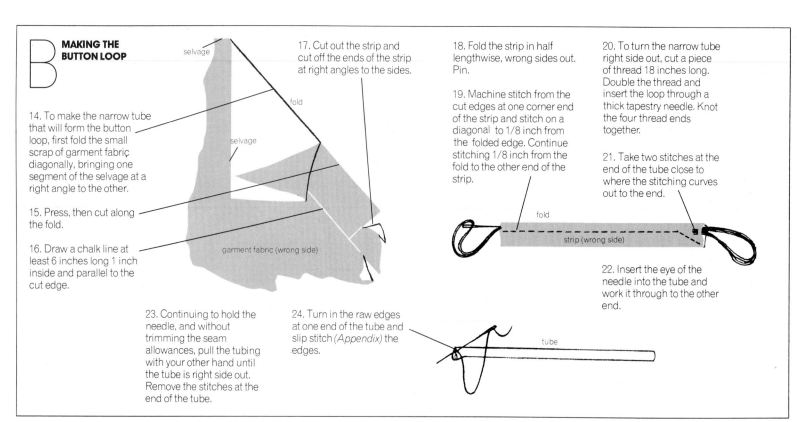

23. Continuing to hold the needle, and without trimming the seam allowances, pull the tubing with your other hand until the tube is right side out. Remove the stitches at the end of the tube.

24. Turn in the raw edges at one end of the tube and slip stitch (Appendix) the edges.

C FINISHING THE DJELLABA

25. Sew a button to the left garment front at the neck edge.

26. Fold the tube into a loop and hold the ends of the tube on the right garment front. Then adjust the loop around the button by holding the finished end of the tube 1/2 inch inside the neckline edge on the right garment front, and pulling on the unfinished end.

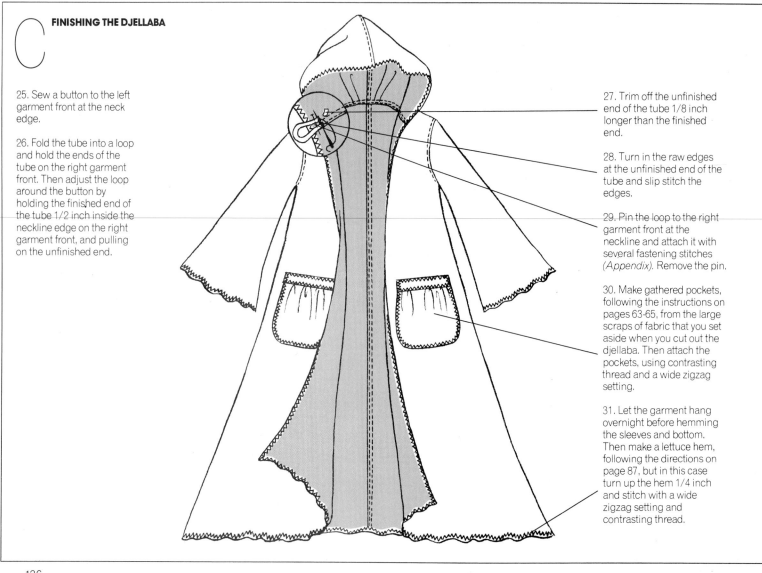

27. Trim off the unfinished end of the tube 1/8 inch longer than the finished end.

28. Turn in the raw edges at the unfinished end of the tube and slip stitch the edges.

29. Pin the loop to the right garment front at the neckline and attach it with several fastening stitches (Appendix). Remove the pin.

30. Make gathered pockets, following the instructions on pages 63-65, from the large scraps of fabric that you set aside when you cut out the djellaba. Then attach the pockets, using contrasting thread and a wide zigzag setting.

31. Let the garment hang overnight before hemming the sleeves and bottom. Then make a lettuce hem, following the directions on page 87, but in this case turn up the hem 1/4 inch and stitch with a wide zigzag setting and contrasting thread.

MAKING THE PATTERN FOR THE REVERSIBLE BIKINI

A TAKING YOUR MEASUREMENTS

1. To prepare the special pattern for the bikini top, measure down across the tip of your bust from the desired position of the upper edge of the bikini top to just below the bottom of your bust.

2. Measure your bustline around the fullest part.

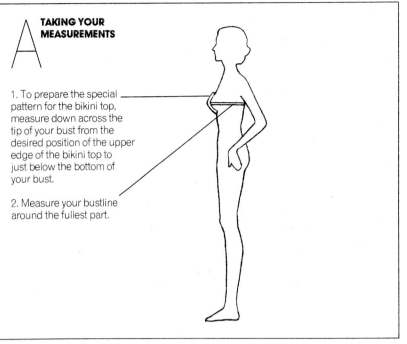

B MAKING THE BIKINI TOP PATTERN

3. Add 2 inches to the measurement determined in Step 1.

4. Divide in half the measurement determined in Step 2, then add 10 inches.

5. On paper, draw a rectangle the length and width found in Steps 3 and 4.

6. Mark the center of one short side of the rectangle.

7. Draw a line inside the rectangle 10 inches from the marked side and parallel to it.

8. On the line drawn in Step 7 make a mark 1 inch below the top of the rectangle and another 1 inch above the bottom of the rectangle.

9. Mark on both the top and bottom lines the midway point between the line drawn in Step 7 and the unmarked side of the rectangle.

10. Using a curved ruler, connect the top mark made in Step 9 with the mark made in Step 8.

11. To finish the curved upper seam line of the bikini top, align the long gradual curve on the ruler with the mark made in Step 6 and the curved line drawn in Step 10. Then draw a curved line that tapers smoothly into the first curved line.

12. Turn the curved ruler over and repeat Steps 10 and 11 to draw the lower seam line.

13. Label the right-hand side of the rectangle "fold line."

14. Cut out the pattern.

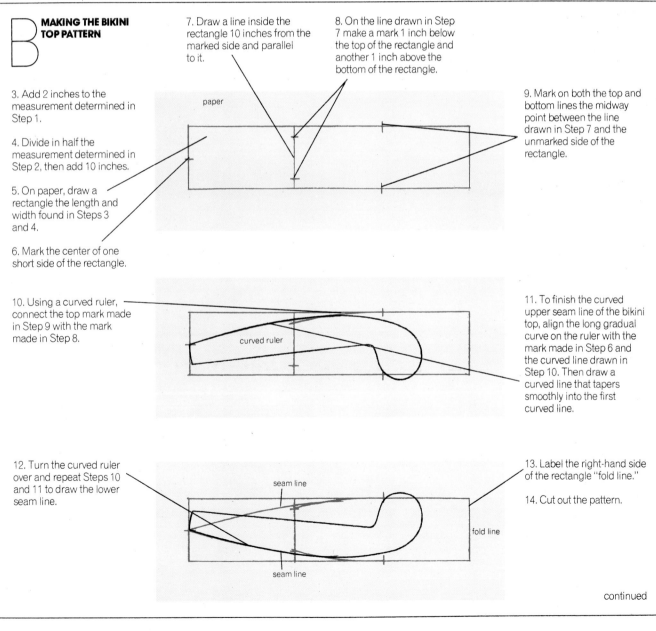

continued

CUTTING AND MARKING THE BIKINI

A   DETERMINING FABRIC REQUIREMENTS

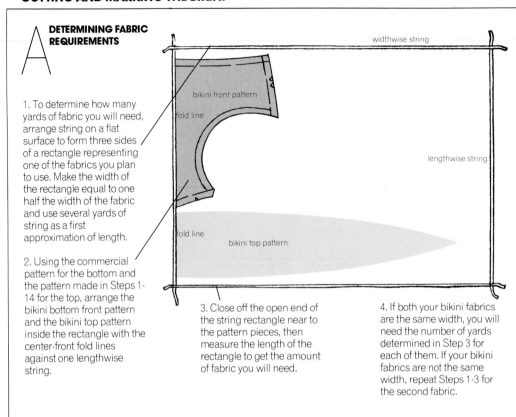

1. To determine how many yards of fabric you will need, arrange string on a flat surface to form three sides of a rectangle representing one of the fabrics you plan to use. Make the width of the rectangle equal to one half the width of the fabric and use several yards of string as a first approximation of length.

2. Using the commercial pattern for the bottom and the pattern made in Steps 1-14 for the top, arrange the bikini bottom front pattern and the bikini top pattern inside the rectangle with the center-front fold lines against one lengthwise string.

3. Close off the open end of the string rectangle near to the pattern pieces, then measure the length of the rectangle to get the amount of fabric you will need.

4. If both your bikini fabrics are the same width, you will need the number of yards determined in Step 3 for each of them. If your bikini fabrics are not the same width, repeat Steps 1-3 for the second fabric.

B   CUTTING AND MARKING

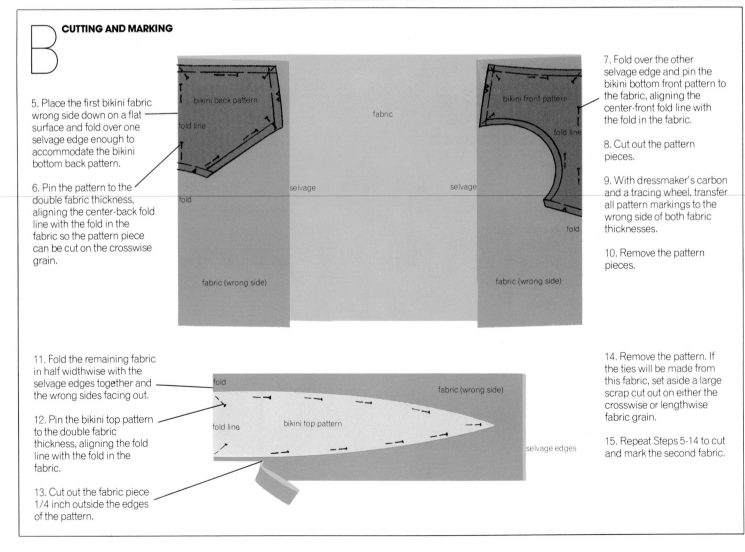

5. Place the first bikini fabric wrong side down on a flat surface and fold over one selvage edge enough to accommodate the bikini bottom back pattern.

6. Pin the pattern to the double fabric thickness, aligning the center-back fold line with the fold in the fabric so the pattern piece can be cut on the crosswise grain.

7. Fold over the other selvage edge and pin the bikini bottom front pattern to the fabric, aligning the center-front fold line with the fold in the fabric.

8. Cut out the pattern pieces.

9. With dressmaker's carbon and a tracing wheel, transfer all pattern markings to the wrong side of both fabric thicknesses.

10. Remove the pattern pieces.

11. Fold the remaining fabric in half widthwise with the selvage edges together and the wrong sides facing out.

12. Pin the bikini top pattern to the double fabric thickness, aligning the fold line with the fold in the fabric.

13. Cut out the fabric piece 1/4 inch outside the edges of the pattern.

14. Remove the pattern. If the ties will be made from this fabric, set aside a large scrap cut out on either the crosswise or lengthwise fabric grain.

15. Repeat Steps 5-14 to cut and mark the second fabric.

ASSEMBLING THE BIKINI

A STITCHING THE BIKINI BOTTOM

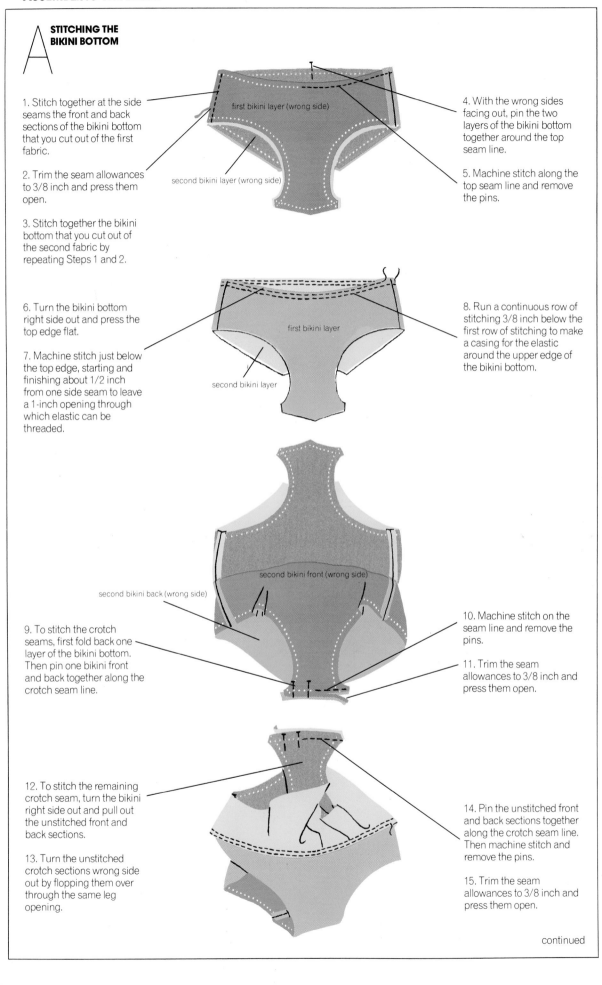

1. Stitch together at the side seams the front and back sections of the bikini bottom that you cut out of the first fabric.

2. Trim the seam allowances to 3/8 inch and press them open.

3. Stitch together the bikini bottom that you cut out of the second fabric by repeating Steps 1 and 2.

first bikini layer (wrong side)

second bikini layer (wrong side)

4. With the wrong sides facing out, pin the two layers of the bikini bottom together around the top seam line.

5. Machine stitch along the top seam line and remove the pins.

6. Turn the bikini bottom right side out and press the top edge flat.

7. Machine stitch just below the top edge, starting and finishing about 1/2 inch from one side seam to leave a 1-inch opening through which elastic can be threaded.

first bikini layer

second bikini layer

8. Run a continuous row of stitching 3/8 inch below the first row of stitching to make a casing for the elastic around the upper edge of the bikini bottom.

second bikini back (wrong side)

second bikini front (wrong side)

9. To stitch the crotch seams, first fold back one layer of the bikini bottom. Then pin one bikini front and back together along the crotch seam line.

10. Machine stitch on the seam line and remove the pins.

11. Trim the seam allowances to 3/8 inch and press them open.

12. To stitch the remaining crotch seam, turn the bikini right side out and pull out the unstitched front and back sections.

13. Turn the unstitched crotch sections wrong side out by flopping them over through the same leg opening.

14. Pin the unstitched front and back sections together along the crotch seam line. Then machine stitch and remove the pins.

15. Trim the seam allowances to 3/8 inch and press them open.

continued

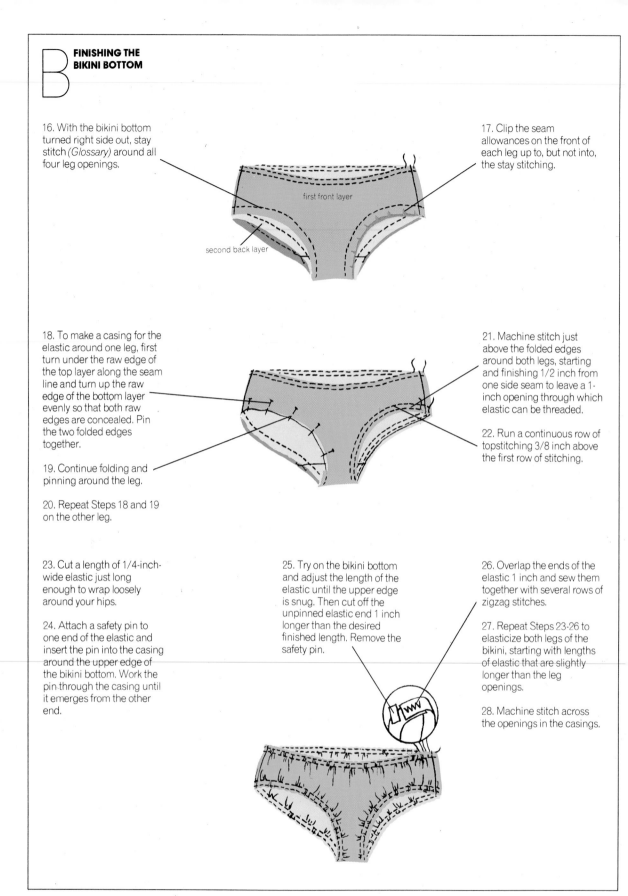

16. With the bikini bottom turned right side out, stay stitch *(Glossary)* around all four leg openings.

first front layer

second back layer

17. Clip the seam allowances on the front of each leg up to, but not into, the stay stitching.

18. To make a casing for the elastic around one leg, first turn under the raw edge of the top layer along the seam line and turn up the raw edge of the bottom layer evenly so that both raw edges are concealed. Pin the two folded edges together.

19. Continue folding and pinning around the leg.

20. Repeat Steps 18 and 19 on the other leg.

21. Machine stitch just above the folded edges around both legs, starting and finishing 1/2 inch from one side seam to leave a 1-inch opening through which elastic can be threaded.

22. Run a continuous row of topstitching 3/8 inch above the first row of stitching.

23. Cut a length of 1/4-inch-wide elastic just long enough to wrap loosely around your hips.

24. Attach a safety pin to one end of the elastic and insert the pin into the casing around the upper edge of the bikini bottom. Work the pin through the casing until it emerges from the other end.

25. Try on the bikini bottom and adjust the length of the elastic until the upper edge is snug. Then cut off the unpinned elastic end 1 inch longer than the desired finished length. Remove the safety pin.

26. Overlap the ends of the elastic 1 inch and sew them together with several rows of zigzag stitches.

27. Repeat Steps 23-26 to elasticize both legs of the bikini, starting with lengths of elastic that are slightly longer than the leg openings.

28. Machine stitch across the openings in the casings.

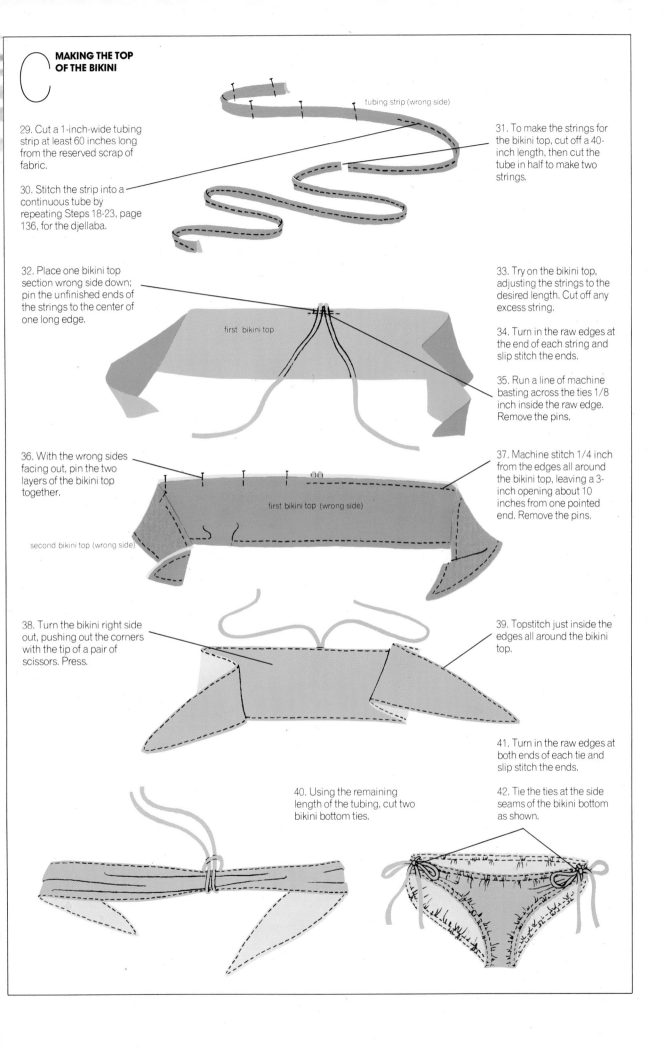

29. Cut a 1-inch-wide tubing strip at least 60 inches long from the reserved scrap of fabric.

30. Stitch the strip into a continuous tube by repeating Steps 18-23, page 136, for the djellaba.

tubing strip (wrong side)

31. To make the strings for the bikini top, cut off a 40-inch length, then cut the tube in half to make two strings.

32. Place one bikini top section wrong side down; pin the unfinished ends of the strings to the center of one long edge.

first bikini top

33. Try on the bikini top, adjusting the strings to the desired length. Cut off any excess string.

34. Turn in the raw edges at the end of each string and slip stitch the ends.

35. Run a line of machine basting across the ties 1/8 inch inside the raw edge. Remove the pins.

36. With the wrong sides facing out, pin the two layers of the bikini top together.

second bikini top (wrong side)

first bikini top (wrong side)

37. Machine stitch 1/4 inch from the edges all around the bikini top, leaving a 3-inch opening about 10 inches from one pointed end. Remove the pins.

38. Turn the bikini right side out, pushing out the corners with the tip of a pair of scissors. Press.

39. Topstitch just inside the edges all around the bikini top.

41. Turn in the raw edges at both ends of each tie and slip stitch the ends.

40. Using the remaining length of the tubing, cut two bikini bottom ties.

42. Tie the ties at the side seams of the bikini bottom as shown.

5
STITCHES FOR QUICK-CHANGE ARTISTRY

Once the province of tweedy matrons, bronzed skiers and gnarled fishermen, hand-knitted and crocheted garments have become a favored part of the wardrobe of experienced travelers. "We live in a casual world," says designer Constance Montgomery, who employs a group of cottage industry artisans to turn out the hand knits and crochets she produces exclusively for the collections of Bill Blass. "Sweaters and

UNCRUSHABLE HAND KNITS AND CROCHETS

other knitwear can take a beating. A hand-knitted wardrobe can be mashed into a suitcase and come out springing."

The secret of this springiness is partly in the method of construction, partly in the way the garments are shaped. In knitting and crocheting the yarn comes off the needles or hook in continuous loops that slide and give against each other more readily than in most machine-knit yard goods. There are no crisscrossing intersections, as in woven cloth, to lock the yarn into a rigid structure; whatever stress is placed upon the fabric is distributed evenly through the network of stitches.

But the main reason hand knits and crochets remain crease-free through hours of wear or packing is the fact that their shape is built in. First, they are given their contours as the fabric is formed, right under the needle or hook. That shape is fixed by blocking. Whether dampened, patted and stretched into the desired dimensions, or pinned into shape and set with a steam iron, blocking gives the yarn a permanent crimp, locking each loop into position. Whenever the garment is cleaned or laundered, the loops return to their original position and the garment regains its shape as it dries.

Hand knits and crochets offer advantages of style and practicality. Since the fabric, not just the garment, is individually made, the coordination of color and texture so essential to travel separates is possible. One maker offers 46 colors, four yarn weights and a choice of all-wool or all-acrylic yarns, as well as wool and acrylic blends.

Combining both knitting and crochet, the six-piece outfit on the following pages is made in a trio of earthy hues. Three of its parts—a tunic, a skirt and a voluminous scarf—are knitted; three others—a wraparound coat, a hat and a matching purse—are worked in afghan crochet. Sometimes known as Tunisian crochet or tricot crochet, the stitch has a hybrid nature. It looks a bit like knitting (hence its name tricot, the French word for knit), and it is made on a hook that resembles a knitting needle.

The fringed scarf is knitted on conventional straight needles, but the tunic and skirt are made on circular ones, all but eliminating the need for seams, and making use of the reversible design. A circular needle is easier and faster to use than two needles; the stitch remains constant instead of shifting from knit to purl. Also, a circular needle minimizes the problem of keeping yarn tension even. Unvarying tension is important for travel garments; unevenness can create loops that catch and pull on any rough surface the garment brushes against.

Working with yarn held under even tension is essential to the fit of hand-crafted clothes. If the stitches are too tight, the garment will be, too; if they are loose, the garment will lack resiliency and lose its shape. The best way to assure even tension is to check and recheck the number of stitches in an inch as the project proceeds—especially after working a while, since fatigue can lead to a tightening or loosening of the fingers. Mindful of these problems, knitwear designer Constance Montgomery regularly sends a pattern of the finished garment to the women who knit and crochet for her, so they can measure their work against it.

A hand-knit sweater set by Mrs. Montgomery is expensive; women who buy her things undoubtedly think of them as long-term investments, to be worn through many seasons. The average home knitter or crocheter could probably duplicate all five parts of the multipurpose wardrobe on the following pages for less than a third the cost of similar garments bought in a store.

Knitting turnabout

Pierced by the two kinds of needles on which they were knitted, the pattern swatches at left are designed to be used either side out. The tubular patterns made on the circular needle have been knitted to show both sides at once in the photograph, while the straight-needle flat swatches have simply been twisted to show their pattern reverse.

The reversible knits, left to right, are a two-color horizontal design, a vertical stripe, a tricolor stockinette, a two-color post-and-rail tweed and a two-color lattice tweed.

Instructions for making the knitted patterns

To make the circular and straight knitted patterns pictured on the preceding pages, you will need knitting worsted weight yarn in three colors, a pair of Size 8 straight knitting needles and a Size 8 circular needle.

The circular needle is a slender, flexible cable with metal or plastic points—like those of straight needles—at both ends.

Knitting on a circular needle differs from conventional knitting on straight needles in only two ways: when the original cast-on foundation stitches are completed, they are joined to form a continuous round. Then all subsequent rows are worked around and around, rather than back and forth, to produce seamless garments.

The illustrations that accompany the instructions show how to use the circular needle. All other basic knitting stitches and techniques are in the Appendix.

All of the swatches are worked in a gauge of 5 stitches to the inch. To check the gauge, knit a sample swatch that measures at least 4 inches square on straight needles, 4 inches long on a circular needle. Lay the swatch on a flat surface and count the number of stitches to the inch—using a ruler, rather than a tape measure, for accuracy. If the gauge requires more stitches to the inch, change to a smaller needle; for fewer stitches to the inch, use a larger needle.

THE TWO-COLOR HORIZONTAL DESIGN PATTERN

Using a circular needle, hold one pointed end firmly in your right hand. Ignoring the other pointed end for the moment, and using color A yarn (dark blue in the photograph on pages 146-147), cast on any desired number of stitches that is a multiple of four. Make sure to cast on enough stitches so that when joining the stitches into a round you will be able to slide them easily onto the other point of the needle. Place a marker on the right-hand end of the needle by tying a piece of contrasting color yarn around the point to indicate the end of one round and the beginning of the next. Now position the needle so that it forms a circle; hold the point of the needle where the last cast-on stitch is located in your right hand, and the point of the needle with the first cast-on stitch in your left hand. Check the stitches to make sure they are not twisted on the needle. Next, join the last cast-on stitch to the first stitch you made in the following manner: insert the tip of the needle in your right hand into the first cast-on stitch on the other point of

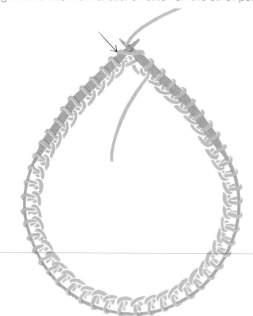

the needle as if to knit (drawing above, arrow). Now bring the yarn over the right-hand end of the needle as if to knit (drawing above), and draw the yarn through the stitch. Be very careful to pull the yarn taut to prevent a gap between the joined stitches.

Round 1: Continuing to use color A yarn, knit each stitch around, pulling the first stitch very tight to prevent any separation at the join, and checking again to be sure the stitches are not twisted. When you reach the marker indicating the end of the round, simply slide the marker off the left-hand point of the needle onto the right-hand.

Repeat this procedure at the end of each successive round throughout.

Round 2: Repeat round 1.

Round 3: Join color B yarn (light blue in the photograph), and knit 1 stitch. Bring the yarn in front of the work as if to purl, then slip 1 stitch as if to purl. Return the yarn to the back of the work, then repeat this sequence— knit 1 stitch, yarn in front, slip 1 stitch—around.

Round 4: Repeat round 3, continuing to use color B.

Round 5: Pick up the color A yarn. Knit each stitch around.

Round 6: Repeat round 5, continuing to use color A.

Round 7: Pick up the color B yarn again and bring the yarn in front of the work as if to purl. Slip 1 stitch as if to purl, then knit 1 stitch. Repeat this sequence— yarn in front, slip 1 stitch as if to purl, knit 1 stitch— around.

Round 8: Repeat round 7, continuing to use color B.

Repeat the preceding 8 rounds as many times as desired. Then bind off.

THE VERTICAL STRIPE PATTERN

Using a circular needle, follow the instructions for casting on and joining the stitches into a round for the two-color horizontal design pattern *(left)*, again making sure the stitches are not twisted on the needle. Place a marker on the right-hand end of the needle as directed for that pattern.

Round 1: Knit 2 stitches, then purl 2 stitches. Repeat this sequence of knitting 2 stitches, then purling 2 stitches around until you reach the marker indicating the end of this round. Slide the marker from the left to the right-hand point as instructed for the two-color horizontal design pattern *(left)*, and do this at the end of each round.

Round 2: Purl each stitch around.

Repeat the preceding 2 rounds as many times as desired. Then bind off.

THE TRICOLOR STOCKINETTE PATTERN

Using a circular needle and color A yarn (maroon in the photograph on pages 146-147), follow the instructions for casting on and joining the stitches into a round for the two-color horizontal design pattern *(left)*, placing a yarn marker on the right-hand end of the needle as directed for that pattern.

Round 1: Knit each stitch around until you reach the marker indicating the end of this round. Slide the marker from the left to the right-hand end of the needle as instructed for the two-color horizontal design pattern, and do this at the end of each round.

Round 2: Repeat round 1.

Round 3: Join color C yarn (light brown in the photograph) and knit 1 stitch. Attach color B yarn (pink in the photograph) and knit 1 stitch. Repeat this sequence— knit 1 stitch with color C, knit 1 stitch with color B— around.

Round 4: Repeat round 3, continuing to work with color C and color B in the appropriate order.

Round 5: Pick up the color A yarn. Knit each stitch around.

Round 6: Repeat round 5, using color A.

Round 7: Pick up the color C yarn and knit 2 stitches. Pick up the color B yarn and knit 1 stitch. Then pick up color C again and knit 3 stitches. Repeat this sequence— knit 1 stitch with color B, then knit 3 stitches with color C. End the round by knitting the last stitch with color C.

Round 8: Repeat round 7, continuing to work with color C and color B in the appropriate order.

Repeat the preceding 8 rounds as many times as desired. Then bind off.

THE POST-AND-RAIL TWEED PATTERN

Using a pair of straight knitting needles and color A yarn (light brown in the photograph on pages 146-147), cast on any uneven number of stitches.

Row 1: Knit each stitch across the row, using only color A.

Row 2: Purl each stitch across the row, using only color A.

Row 3: Attach color B yarn (maroon in the photograph) and knit 1 stitch. Then slip 1 stitch as if to purl. Knit 1 stitch. Repeat the following sequence— slip 1 stitch as if to purl, then knit 1 stitch— across the row, ending the row by knitting the last stitch.

Row 4: Still using color B, knit 1 stitch. Bring the yarn in front of the work as if to purl, and slip 1 stitch as if to purl. Knit the next stitch. Repeat this sequence— yarn in front, slip 1 stitch, knit 1 stitch— across the row. Knit the last stitch.

Repeat the preceding 4 rows as many times as desired. Then bind off.

THE TWO-COLOR LATTICE TWEED PATTERN

Using a pair of straight knitting needles and color A yarn (light blue in the photograph on pages 146-147), cast on any uneven number of stitches.

Row 1: Purl each stitch across the row, using only color A.

Row 2: Knit each stitch across the row, using only color A.

Row 3: Attach color B yarn (light brown in the photograph). Purl 1 stitch. Then slip 1 stitch as if to purl. Repeat the following sequence— purl 1 stitch, slip 1 stitch as if to purl — across the row, ending the row by purling the last stitch.

Row 4: Still using color B, knit 1 stitch. Slip 1 stitch as if to knit. Repeat this sequence— knit 1 stitch, slip 1 stitch — across the row. Knit the last stitch.

Row 5: Pick up color A. Purl each stitch across the row.

Row 6: Still using color A, knit each stitch across the row.

Row 7: Slip the first stitch as if to purl. Pick up color B, then purl 1 stitch. Repeat the following sequence— slip 1 stitch, purl 1 stitch— across the row. End by slipping the last stitch as if to purl.

Row 8: To begin this row, slip the first stitch as if to knit. Still using color B, knit 1 stitch. Repeat this sequence— slip 1 stitch as if to knit, then knit 1 stitch— across the row, ending the row by slipping the last stitch as if to knit.

Repeat the preceding 8 rows as many times as desired. Then bind off.

Two-faced crochet

Twisted to show how they look on both sides, the swatches displayed on these pages are worked in variants of afghan crochet stitches that are designed to be used for making reversible garments. Afghan stitch crochet requires the use of a special elongated crochet hook and is worked in two parts: first, the stitches are picked up on the hook, in the fashion of knitting; then they are worked off, to complete the row, as in conventional crochet.

The afghan patterns, left to right, are a twisted afghan stitch, a two-color basic afghan stitch, a two-color vertical bar stitch, a solid-color afghan stitch, and a two-color stockinette stitch.

Instructions for making the afghan stitch patterns

To make the afghan stitch patterns pictured on the preceding pages, you will need knitting worsted-weight yarn in two colors and a Size K aluminum afghan hook.

As in regular crochet, afghan stitch crochet starts with a foundation chain. The stitches are worked in basically the same manner as crochet stitches—that is, the yarn is brought over the hook, then drawn through loops. Each row of afghan crochet, however, is worked in two parts. On the first part, working from right to left, all the stitches are picked up and held on the hook. In the second part, working from left to right, each stitch is worked off the hook to complete the row.

Whatever the pattern you have chosen, row 1 is always worked in the same manner to establish a uniform foundation of vertical bars that can then be worked off in different ways on subsequent rows to provide various design effects. Because the two parts of every row are worked back and forth on the hook, the work is never turned at the end of each row as in conventional crochet, except when shaping garments.

These patterns are worked in a gauge of 4 stitches to the inch. To check the gauge, make a sample swatch that measures at least 4 inches square. Lay the swatch flat and count the number of stitches to the inch, using a ruler—rather than a tape measure—to ensure accuracy. If the gauge requires more stitches to the inch than you have made in the swatch, change to a smaller hook; if the gauge calls for fewer stitches to the inch, use a larger hook. This change of hook size will also alter the row-to-the-inch gauge. Basic crochet stitches and techniques—such as the chain stitch, attaching yarn and fastening off—that you will need for making these patterns are explained in the Appendix. The illustrations that accompany the instructions on these pages show how to use the afghan hook to create the swatch patterns.

THE SOLID-COLOR AFGHAN STITCH PATTERN

Begin the pattern by making a foundation chain of any desired number of stitches.

Row 1: For the first part of this row, start by making 1 chain stitch. Insert the hook in the second chain stitch from the hook; bring the yarn over the hook. Draw the yarn through the stitch to form a second loop on the hook (*drawing 1*). Insert the hook in the next stitch, bring the yarn over and

1

draw it through the stitch, forming three loops on the hook. Repeat this sequence—insert the hook, yarn over and draw through—in each remaining chain stitch across the row, holding all stitches on the hook. At the end of this part of row 1, you will have the same number of stitches on the hook as on the original foundation chain (*drawing 2*). For the second part of this row, start by bringing the yarn over

2

the hook and drawing it through the first loop on the hook (*drawing 3, arrow*). Then bring the yarn over the hook again and draw it through the next two loops on the hook (*drawing 3*). Repeat this sequence—bring the yarn over the hook, then draw it through the next two loops

3

on the hook—until only one loop remains on the hook.

Row 2: For the first part of this row, start by making 1 chain stitch. Skip the first vertical bar. Then insert the hook from right to left under the top strand of the next vertical bar *(drawing 4, arrow)*, bring the yarn over the hook and draw it through. There will now be two loops on the hook. Repeat this sequence—insert the hook underneath, yarn over

4

and draw through—in the top strand of each vertical bar across the row until you reach the last vertical bar at the left-hand end of the work, holding all the stitches on the hook. End this part of row 2 by inserting the hook under both strands of the last vertical bar *(drawing 5, arrow)*. Then place the yarn over the hook and draw it through.

5

You will now have the same number of stitches on the hook that you had on the original foundation chain.
For the second part of row 2, repeat the instructions for the second part of row 1 *(left)* until one loop remains on the hook.
To form the pattern, continue to repeat the first and then the second parts of row 2 as many times as desired.
If you wish to bind off the last row to create a finished edge, make sure you have completed the second part of row 2. Chain 1, and skip the first vertical bar. Insert the hook through the top strand of the next vertical bar. Bring the yarn over the hook and draw it through to form two loops on the hook *(drawing 6)*. Make a slip stitch through the two loops on the hook by bringing the yarn over the hook again,

6

then drawing it through both loops, leaving one loop on the hook. Continue to work in this manner—inserting the hook under the top strand of each vertical bar, bringing the yarn over, drawing it through, bringing the yarn over again and drawing it through the two loops on the hook—until all vertical bars have been worked and one loop remains on the hook. Fasten off. Carefully weave in any loose threads so that they are not visible.

THE TWO-COLOR AFGHAN STITCH PATTERN

Using color A yarn (beige in the photograph on pages 150-151), make a foundation chain of any desired number of stitches.

Row 1: For the first part of this row, repeat the instructions for the first part of row 1 of the solid-color afghan stitch pattern *(opposite page)*.
For the second part of row 1, repeat the instructions for the second part of row 1 of the solid-color afghan stitch pattern up to the point where two loops remain on the hook. Attach color B yarn (royal blue in the photograph) and draw the yarn through the remaining two loops on the hook.

Row 2: For the first part of this row, start by skipping the first color A vertical bar *(drawing 7, arrow)*. Then insert the hook

7

from right to left under the top strand of the next vertical bar, as illustrated in drawing 4, at left. Using color B yarn, bring the yarn over the hook and draw it through, forming two loops on the hook *(drawing 7)*. Repeat this sequence—insert the hook underneath, yarn over and draw it through—in the top strand of each successive vertical bar across the row, holding all stitches on the hook, until you reach the last vertical bar at the left-hand end of the work. End this part of row 2 by inserting the hook under both strands of the last color A vertical bar *(drawing 8, arrow)*,

8

then bring the yarn over the hook and draw it through. You will now have the same number of color B stitches on the hook as on the original foundation chain.
For the second part of row 2, repeat the instructions for the second part of row 2 of the solid-color afghan stitch pattern *(left)* until two loops remain on the hook. Pick up the color A yarn again, then bring the yarn over the hook and draw it through the two remaining loops.
To form the pattern, continue to repeat the first and then the second parts of row 2 as many times as desired, making sure to alternate color A and color B yarn each time you begin the first part of the row.
If you wish to bind off the last row of your work to create a finished edge, make sure you have completed the second part of row 2 to the point where two loops remain on the hook. Continuing to use the same color yarn you are working with at this point, bring the yarn over the hook and draw it through both loops on the hook. Chain 1, then bind off the edge with slip stitches following the instructions for binding off the solid-color afghan stitch pattern *(left)*, be-

ginning with skipping the first vertical bar and making the slip stitches through the top strands of each vertical bar across the row as you did for the pattern. Fasten off. Carefully weave in any loose threads so that they will not be visible.

THE TWO-COLOR VERTICAL BAR PATTERN

Using color A yarn (royal blue in the photograph on pages 150-151), begin the pattern by making a foundation chain of any desired number of stitches.

Row 1: For the first part of this row, repeat the instructions for the first part of row 1 of the solid-color afghan stitch pattern *(page 152)*.

For the second part of row 1, repeat the instructions for the second part of row 1 of the solid-color afghan stitch pattern until two loops remain on the hook. Attach color B yarn (olive green in the photograph), and draw the yarn through the remaining two loops on the hook.

Row 2: For the first part of this row, start by skipping the first color A vertical bar. Then insert the hook in the space before the next vertical bar *(drawing 9, arrow)*. Using color B, bring the yarn over the hook and draw it through the space, forming two loops on the hook.

9

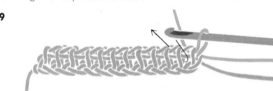

Repeat this sequence—insert the hook in the space before the next vertical bar, yarn over and draw it through the space—before each vertical bar across the row, holding all the stitches on the hook. At the end of this part of the row, you will have the same number of color B stitches on the hook that you had on the original foundation chain.

For the second part of row 2, repeat the instructions for the second part of row 2 of the solid-color afghan stitch pattern *(page 153)* until two loops remain on the hook. Pick up the color A yarn again, then bring the yarn over the hook and draw it through the two remaining loops *(drawing 10)*.

Row 3: For the first part of this row, begin by skipping the first and second color B vertical bars. Then insert the crochet

10

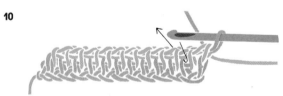

hook in the space between the next two color B vertical bars *(drawing 10, arrow)*. Using the color A yarn, bring the yarn over the hook and draw it through the space. Repeat this sequence—inserting the hook in the space between the next two vertical bars, bringing the yarn over the hook and drawing it through—in each space across the row, holding all the stitches on the hook. At the end of this part of row 3, insert the hook in the last color B stitch of the row

(drawing 11, arrow), then bring the yarn over the hook and draw it through the stitch. You will now have the same number of color A stitches on the hook that you had on the original foundation chain.

For the second part of row 3, repeat the instructions for the

11

second part of row 2 of the solid-color afghan stitch pattern *(page 153)* until two loops remain on the hook. Pick up the color B yarn again, then bring the yarn over the hook and draw it through the two remaining loops.

To form the pattern, continue to repeat the first and then the second parts of row 2, followed by the first and then the second parts of row 3 as many times as desired. Make sure to start the first part of each even-numbered row by picking up the color B yarn, and to start the first part of each odd-numbered row by picking up the color A yarn.

If you wish to bind off the last row of your work to create a finished edge, make sure you have completed the second part of row 3 to the point where two loops remain on the hook. Continuing to use the same color yarn you are working with at this point, bring the yarn over the hook and draw it through both loops on the hook. Chain 1, then bind off the edge with slip stitches following the instructions for binding off the solid-color afghan stitch pattern *(page 153)*, beginning with skipping the first vertical bar and this time making the slip stitches through the spaces between each successive vertical bar across the row as you did for the pattern. Fasten off. Carefully weave in any loose threads so that they are not visible.

THE TWISTED AFGHAN STITCH PATTERN

Begin the pattern by making a foundation chain of any multiple of 2 chain stitches plus 1 chain stitch.

Row 1: For the first part of this row, repeat the instructions for the first part of row 1 of the solid-color afghan stitch pattern *(page 152)*.

For the second part of this row, repeat the instructions for the second part of row 1 of the solid-color afghan stitch pattern.

Row 2: For the first part of this row, start by making 1 chain stitch. Then skip the first and second vertical bars *(drawing 12, double arrow)*. Next insert the hook from right to left under the top strand of the next vertical bar, bring the yarn over the hook and draw it through, creating two loops on the hook *(drawing 12)*. Now return to the second vertical bar you skipped *(drawing 12, bottom arrow)* and insert the

12

hook from right to left under the top strand of this vertical bar. Bring the yarn over the hook and draw it through. Skip the next unworked vertical bar—it will be the fourth vertical bar of the row—and insert the hook from right to left under the top strand of the next vertical bar after the one you skipped. Bring the yarn over the hook and draw it through, creating four loops on the hook. Return to the last vertical bar you just skipped, insert the hook under the top strand of this vertical bar, then bring the yarn over the hook and draw it through. Continue to work in this manner —skipping the next unworked vertical bar, working the top strand of the next vertical bar after the one you skipped in the established way, returning to work the skipped vertical bar—until all top strands of each vertical bar of the row have been worked. Hold all stitches on the hook. The last stitch of the row will be in the next-to-last vertical bar from the left-hand end of the work (drawing 13, arrow). You will now have the same number of stitches on the hook that you had on the original foundation chain.

13

For the second part of row 2, repeat the instructions for the second part of row 2 of the solid-color afghan stitch pattern (page 153).

To form the pattern, repeat the first and then the second parts of row 2 as many times as desired.

If you would like to bind off the last row of your work to create a finished edge, make sure you have completed the second part of row 2. Chain 1, then bind off the edge of the work with slip stitches following the instructions for binding off the solid-color afghan stitch pattern (page 153), but this time beginning with skipping the first two vertical bars and making the first slip stitch through the top strand of the next vertical bar, then returning to the second vertical bar and making a slip stitch through the top strand of this bar (drawing 14). Continue to skip the next unworked vertical bar, then work a slip stitch through the next vertical bar (drawing 14, arrow), then return to the skipped vertical bar, working a slip stitch through it, until all the top strands

14

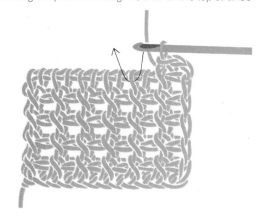

of the vertical bars of the row have been worked. Fasten off. Carefully weave in any loose threads so that they are not visible.

THE STOCKINETTE STITCH PATTERN

Using color A yarn (emerald green in the photograph on pages 150-151), begin the pattern by making a foundation chain of any desired number of stitches.

Row 1: For the first part of this row, repeat the instructions for the first part of row 1 of the solid-color afghan stitch pattern (page 152).

For the second part of this row, repeat the instructions for the second part of row 1 of the solid-color afghan stitch pattern until there are two loops remaining on the hook. Now attach color B yarn (lime green in the photograph), and draw it through the remaining two loops on the hook (drawing 15).

Row 2: For the first part of this row, begin by skipping the first

15

vertical bar, then insert the hook between the strands of the next vertical bar (drawing 15, arrow). Using color B, bring the yarn over the hook and draw it through, forming two loops on the hook. Repeat this sequence—insert the hook between the strands of the next vertical bar, bring the yarn over the hook and draw it through the strands—in each vertical bar across the row, holding all the stitches on the hook. You will now have the same number of color B stitches on the hook that you had on the original foundation chain.

For the second part of row 2, repeat the instructions for the second part of row 2 of the solid-color afghan stitch pattern (page 153) until two loops remain on the hook. Pick up the color A yarn again, then bring the yarn over the hook and draw it through the two remaining loops, as illustrated in drawing 10 (opposite page).

To form the pattern, continue to repeat the first and then the second parts of row 2 as many times as desired, making sure to alternate color A and color B yarn each time you begin the first part of the row.

If you wish to bind off the last row of your work to create a finished edge, make sure you have completed the second part of row 2 to the point where two loops remain on the hook.

Continuing to use the same color yarn you are working with at this point, bring the yarn over the hook and draw it through both loops on the hook. Chain 1, then bind off the edge with slip stitches following the instructions for binding off the solid-color afghan stitch pattern (page 153), beginning by skipping the first vertical bar and this time making the slip stitches between the strands of each vertical bar across the row as on the pattern. Fasten off. Carefully weave in any loose threads so that they are not visible on either side.

A totally reversible look for traveling

These two swashbuckling woolen ensembles are actually the same knit and crochet clothes and accessories turned inside out. Tunic, skirt, shawl, wrap coat—even the hat and shoulder bag—are reversible, making the outfit not only practical, but versatile. The possibilities for mixing and matching the patterns and layers are almost as astonishing as the low cost; the entire wardrobe can be made for under $100 worth of yarn. Directions for the knit skirt, tunic and shawl begin overleaf; those for the afghan crochet coat, hat and bag begin on page 163.

Instructions for making the knit costume

The knitted skirt, tunic top and shawl are shown twice at left—once on one side, then again on the other—to demonstrate their complete reversibility. The garments can be worn together, as in these photographs, or as separates with other clothes.

In the instructions that follow, the directions for the skirt and the top are written for a size 8; any changes needed for making them in sizes 10, 12, 14 and 16 follow in parentheses, in that order. The shawl is designed to measure approximately 29 inches wide and 96 inches long, with 10-inch fringe knotted at each end. The amount of yarn required is specified immediately preceding each set of instructions.

The skirt is worked on a circular needle in the two-color horizontal design pattern on pages 146-147. The top is also worked on a circular needle, in the tricolor stockinette pattern. The shawl (made on straight needles in the two-color post-and-rail pattern) combines three colors of yarn to create the design. Either of the other two circular swatch patterns or the alternate straight one may be substituted for these garments.

Whichever pattern you choose, work in a gauge of 6 stitches to the inch. Basic knitting stitches and techniques—such as slipping stitches and casting on—are shown in the Appendix.

THE CIRCULAR SKIRT

To make the skirt you will need 5 (5, 6, 6, 7) two-ounce skeins of sport-weight yarn in color A (beige in the skirt shown at left) and 2 (2, 3, 3, 3) two-ounce skeins of sport-weight yarn in color B (light brown at left); a 29-inch-long Size 5 circular knitting needle and a Size E aluminum crochet hook. You will also need a strip of 3/4-inch-wide waistband elastic cut to fit your waist measurement.

The skirt is designed to be mid-calf length. To adjust the length, simply add or subtract the necessary amount between the last of the decreases for the bottom of the skirt and those that are made to shape the waist.

Using color A, start the skirt at the bottom by casting on 276 (288, 300, 312, 324) stitches, placing a yarn marker on the right-hand end of the needle and joining the stitches into a round as instructed for the swatch patterns (pages 148-149).

Following the instructions for the two-color horizontal design pattern (page 148), begin round 1 of the pattern and work across the first 46 (48, 50, 52, 54) stitches. Place a marker on the needle as you did before you joined the stitches into a round. Repeat this sequence—work across the next 46 (48, 50, 52, 54) stitches, then place a marker —five times more. When you have completed the last group of 46 (48, 50, 52, 54) stitches, you will have reached the original yarn marker you placed at the beginning of the round.

Work even in the pattern now—making sure to slip the markers from the left to the right-hand end of the needle —until you have completed three complete pattern sequences (24 rounds in all), ending with round 8.

Shaping the skirt: Continuing to work in the pattern stitch sequence, and beginning with round 1, decrease 1 stitch before and after each marker. You will have made 12 decreases on this round. Repeat the decreases before and after each marker on round 2, making 12 more decreases. You will have 252 (264, 276, 288, 300) stitches remaining on the needle.

Now work even for 24 rounds (three more complete pattern sequences), again ending with round 8. Begin round 1 once more and make the 12 decreases before and after each marker, then work round 2. Make sure to work the decreases in the same manner that you did when you reached the end of the first 24 rounds. There will now be 228 (240, 252, 264, 276) stitches remaining on the needle.

Continue to work now in the established sequence —making three complete pattern stitch sequences, then decreasing 24 stitches on rounds 1 and 2 of the next pattern sequence—until 180 (192, 204, 216, 228) stitches remain on the needle.

At this point, determine how long or short you wish your completed skirt to be. For a 30-inch-long mid-calf-length skirt, work even in the pattern for 25 1/2 inches—3 inches less than the finished length, not including the waistband. For a shorter skirt, subtract the necessary number of inches. If you wish to make a longer one, add as many inches as you need. Make sure to end with round 8 of the pattern.

Shaping the waist: Working on the 180 (192, 204, 216, 228) stitches on the needle, begin round 1 of the pattern stitch sequence and decrease 1 stitch before and after the second, fourth and sixth markers only. Then work round 2, decreasing at the same points you did in round 1. Complete this entire pattern stitch sequence, but now without decreasing.

Then work two more complete pattern stitch sequences, making sure to decrease before and after the same markers on rounds 1 and 2 of each sequence. You will have made 36 decreases in all, and 144 (156, 168, 180, 192) stitches will remain on the needle.

Making the waistband: Drop color B yarn now. Working with color A yarn only, purl around for 1 1/4 inches, then knit around for another 1 1/4 inches. Bind off. Cut a strip of 3/4-inch-wide elastic to fit your waist measurement and sew the short ends of the elastic strip together to form a circle. Place the elastic on the underside of the 2 1/2-inch-long purl/knit waistband of the skirt, then fold the waistband to the underside, covering the elastic. Hem the bound-off edge of the waistband in place.

Finishing the skirt: Block the finished skirt (*Glossary*). Place the skirt with the bottom edge facing up, then work 1 row of single crochet stitches (*Appendix*) around the entire bottom edge, working the stitches through the original cast-on stitches.

Still working with color A and the crochet hook, work 1 row of slip stitches now along each of the six groups of decreases for the bottom of the skirt. Work from the bottom of the skirt upwards, following the vertical lines of the decreases and making the slip stitches through the top only of each color A stitch on the skirt.

To make the crocheted slip stitches, insert the hook from right to left through the top of each knit stitch on the garment. Then bring the yarn over the hook and draw it through the stitch and the loop on the hook. Repeat this procedure in each of the stitches marking the line of decreases.

Turn the skirt to the reverse side and make the same color A slip stitch trim along each line of bottom decreases on this side.

Weave in any loose threads so that they are not visible on either side of the garment.

THE CIRCULAR TUNIC TOP

To make the tunic top you will need 3 (4, 4, 5, 6) two-ounce skeins of sport-weight yarn in color A (rust in the tunic top shown on page 158) and 2 (3, 3, 4, 4) two-ounce skeins of the same yarn in color B and color C (light brown and beige in the tunic top shown). You will also need a 29-inch-long Size 5 circular knitting needle, a pair of Size 5 straight knitting needles and four large stitch holders.

THE MAIN BODY OF THE TOP

Using color A, start the tunic top at the bottom by casting on 180 (192, 204, 216, 228) stitches, placing a yarn marker on the right-hand end of the needle and joining the stitches into a round as you did when making the swatch patterns (*pages 148-149*). Following the instructions for the tricolor stockinette pattern (*page 149*), work even in the pattern stitch, slipping the marker on each round, until the piece measures 19 inches, or the desired length, to the underarm. Make sure you end with either row 2 or row 6 of the pattern.

Now slip 90 (96, 102, 108, 114) stitches onto one of your stitch holders to be worked later for the front yoke, and slip the remaining 90 (96, 102, 108, 114) stitches onto another stitch holder for the back yoke. These stitches will also be worked later.

THE SLEEVES

The right sleeve: Using the straight knitting needles and color A yarn, cast on 36 (36, 40, 40, 44) stitches. Still working in the tricolor stockinette pattern, begin to work the pattern stitch (round 1 now becomes row 1). On round 2—now row 2—reverse the stitches, and rather than knitting them as instructed for the circular pattern swatch, purl each stitch across the row.

Continue to work in the pattern, working each even-numbered row in reverse—that is, using purl stitches where knit stitches are indicated and knit stitches where purl stitches are called for.

Work even in this manner through the 8 rows of one complete pattern stitch sequence. On row 1 of the next pattern sequence, increase 1 stitch at the beginning and end of the row. Work rows 2 to 4 in the established manner—without increasing—then repeat the increase of 1 stitch at the beginning and end of the row on row 5. You will have increased 4 stitches.

Continue to work in the pattern stitch sequence, reversing the stitches on each even-numbered row and increasing 4 stitches on rows 1 and 5 until you have 64 (68, 72, 76, 80) stitches on the needle. Work even on these stitches until the piece measures 17 1/2 inches, or the desired length to the underarm. Make sure to end with either row 2 or row 6 as you did for the body of the tunic top. Place these stitches on a holder to be worked later.

The left sleeve: Work this sleeve in exactly the same manner as the right sleeve, placing the stitches on a holder to be worked later as before.

THE YOKE

Using the circular needle once more, knit across the 90 (96, 102, 108, 114) front yoke stitches from the holder and place a marker on the needle. Then knit across the 64 (68, 72, 76, 80) stitches from the right sleeve holder and place a marker. Now knit across the 90 (96, 102, 108, 114) stitches from the back yoke holder and place a marker. Finally, knit across the 64 (68, 72, 76, 80) stitches from the left sleeve holder and place a marker after you have made these stitches. You will now have 308 (328, 348, 368, 388) stitches on the needle and four markers.

Continuing to work in the pattern stitch—it will be round 3 or round 7, depending on where you ended when you placed the stitches on the holders—work 1 round even on these stitches. On the next round, work rounds 4 or 8 even in the pattern stitch. On the following round—round 5 or 1 of the pattern, which is a color A knit round—make a decrease of 1 stitch before and after each of the four markers.

Repeat this decrease on the next round—round 6 or 2 —and continue working in the pattern stitch sequence, decreasing in the same manner on every color A knit round (every round 1, 2, 5 and 6 of the pattern) until 132 (152, 172, 192, 212) stitches remain. You will have decreased 176 stitches in all. Work even now until the piece measures approximately 7 1/4 (7 1/2, 7 3/4, 8, 8 1/4) inches above the start of the yoke stitches.

Making the collar: Place a marker on the needle to indicate the start of the collar, then continue to work even in the pattern stitch for 3 more inches.

Now, holding the stitches very carefully in place so they do not slip off either end of the needle, turn the entire garment to the reverse side by pulling it through the center of the needle. To make the turn-over collar completely reversible, work even in the pattern stitch sequence for 8 inches more. Bind off.

Finishing the top: Weave the underarm sleeve seams, following the instructions in the Appendix for weaving knitted pieces. Weave the seams first with the dark-colored yarn, catching only the dark-colored stitches; then weave the seam again with the light-colored yarn, catching the light-colored stitches.

Weave in any loose threads so they are not visible on either side.

THE FRINGED SHAWL

To make the shawl, you will need 4 two-ounce skeins of sport-weight yarn in color A (light brown in the shawl shown on page 158), 10 two-ounce skeins of the same yarn in color B (beige in the shawl shown) and 1 skein in color C (rust in the shawl shown). You will also need a pair of Size 7 straight knitting needles and a Size E aluminum crochet hook.

The shawl is worked in the two-color post-and-rail pattern (*page 149*), using different combinations of the three colors of yarn. To create the design, carefully follow the pattern stitch sequence in the swatch instructions, and, at the same time, use the color sequence as directed below. Always end with row 4 of the pattern sequence before beginning the next color sequence.

Using color A yarn, cast on 179 stitches.

The first color sequence: Follow the instructions for the 4 rows of the pattern stitch sequence exactly, using the same color sequence and attaching color B on row 3 as you did for the swatch. Work even in this pattern and color sequence, repeating the 4 rows of the pattern for approximately 7 inches. Make sure that you end with row 4 of the pattern.

The second color sequence: Using only color B, work the pattern stitch sequence for approximately 1 inch, ending with row 4.

The third color sequence: Using colors A and C, work the pattern for approximately 4 inches, remembering throughout that in this sequence the color C stitches are used where the color B stitches are called for in the swatch instructions.

The fourth color sequence: Using color B only, work the pattern for approximately 24 inches.

The fifth color sequence: Using colors A and B, repeat the directions for the first color sequence and work this pattern and color sequence for approximately 14 inches.

The sixth color sequence: Using only color B, repeat the instructions for the second color sequence.

The seventh color sequence: Using colors A and C, repeat the directions for the third color sequence, again remembering to use color C stitches where the color B stitches are called for in the swatch instructions.

The eighth color sequence: Using only color B, repeat the instructions for the second color sequence.

The ninth color sequence: Using colors A and B, repeat the directions for the first color sequence, but work this pattern and color sequence for approximately 4 inches.

The 10th color sequence: Using only color B, repeat the instructions for the fourth color sequence.

The 11th color sequence: Using colors A and B, repeat the directions for the ninth color sequence.

The 12th color sequence: Using only color B, repeat the instructions for the second color sequence.

The 13th color sequence: Using colors A and C, repeat the directions for the third color sequence, but this time work for approximately 7 inches. End with row 4 of the pattern.

The work should now measure approximately 96 inches long. Bind off.

Weave in any loose threads so they are not visible on either side. Block the finished work (*Glossary*).

Finishing the shawl: Work 1 row of single crochet stitches (*Appendix*) along the two long sides and row of cast-on stitches at the bottom of the piece, using color B yarn along all the solid-color B bands and color C on all the other bands.

Making the fringe: Using colors A and B, cut two 20-inch-long strands of each color. Place the strands together, then pull them through the first stitch at either side of one of the short ends of the shawl. Knot the strands around the stitch to make a 10-inch-long length of fringe consisting of eight strands. Repeat this procedure in every other stitch along each short end of the shawl. There will be approximately 85 lengths of fringe at each end.

Instructions for making the afghan crochet ensemble

The two views of the crocheted outfit at left show both sides of the totally reversible afghan stitch wrap coat, hat and shoulder bag. In the instructions that follow, the directions for the coat are written for size 8. Any changes necessary for sizes 10, 12, 14 and 16 follow in parentheses, in that order. The hat is designed to fit all head sizes, and the shoulder bag measures approximately 12 inches square.

For the coat, you will need 5 (5, 6, 6, 7) four-ounce skeins of knitting worsted weight yarn in both color A (rust in the garments shown here) and color B (light brown here). The hat and the shoulder bag each require 1 four-ounce skein of knitting worsted weight yarn in each color. You will also need a Size K aluminum afghan crochet hook.

All three garments are worked in the two-color vertical bar stitch pattern shown in detail in the photograph on pages 150-151, although you may substitute any of the other four patterns shown. Complete instructions for using the afghan hook and making the patterns begin on page 152. Whatever pattern stitch you choose, work in a gauge of 4 stitches to the inch.

The basic crochet stitches and techniques you will need to make these garments—such as the chain stitch and fastening off—are in the Appendix.

THE REVERSIBLE WRAP COAT

THE BACK

Using color A yarn, make a foundation chain of 77 (81, 85, 89, 93) stitches. Following the instructions for the two-color vertical bar stitch pattern that begin on page 154, work even in this pattern stitch for 3 inches, At this point, make sure you are about to begin the first part of either row 2 or row 3 of the pattern.

Now make a decrease of I stitch at the beginning and end of this part of the row, working in the following manner: at the beginning of the row, skip the first vertical bar, then insert the hook under the top strands of the next two vertical bars. Bring the yarn over the hook and draw it through to form two loops on the hook.

Continue to work in the pattern stitch across the row until you reach the third vertical bar from the end. Decrease I stitch as you did at the beginning of the row, but this time insert the hook under the top strands of the third and then the second vertical bar from the end, yarn over and draw through both bars. Work the last stitch of the row as indicated for the pattern—that is, in the last space if you are working on row 2 and in the last stitch if you are working row 3. When you have completed the row, count the number of stitches on the hook to make sure you have 2 stitches less than you had on the original foundation chain.

Continue to work in the pattern stitch, decreasing I stitch at the beginning and end of the first part of the pattern stitch row as you did before, every 3 inches two more times, then every 2 inches three more times. At this point, you will have decreased 12 stitches in all.

Work even now on the 65 (69, 73, 77, 81) remaining stitches until the entire piece measures 29 inches, or the desired length, to the underarm. Place a marker at each side edge of the work to indicate the start of the armhole by tying a small piece of contrasting color yarn through the first and last stitch of the row. Continue to work even in the pattern stitch until the piece measures 8 (8, 8 1/2, 8 1/2, 9) inches above the markers.

Shaping the shoulders: Make sure you are beginning the first part of either afghan stitch pattern row. (On this part of the pattern row, each vertical bar counts as a stitch.) Slip stitch across the first 24 (26, 27, 29, 30) stitches. To do this, insert the hook from right to left through the top strand of the first vertical bar, bring the yarn over the hook and draw it through the bar and the loop on the hook; repeat this procedure in each of the next 23 (25, 26, 28, 29) stitches. Work in the pattern stitch across the next 17 (17, 19, 19, 21) stitches. Chain I, and turn. Work the second part of the afghan stitch pattern row back across the same 17 (17, 19, 19, 21) stitches. Fasten off, without binding off.

THE FRONT

The left front: Using color A yarn, chain 55 (57, 59, 61, 63) stitches. Work even in the pattern stitch for 3 inches. Make sure you are about to begin the first part of the same pattern row as that on which the first decrease was made on the back. Then decrease 1 stitch at the beginning of the row only (it will be the right-hand edge of the work) as you did at the beginning of the row when decreasing on the back of the coat.

Continue to work in the pattern stitch, repeating this decrease every 3 inches two more times, then every 2 inches three more times. You will have decreased 6 stitches in all. Work even now on the 49 (51, 53, 55, 57) remaining stitches until the piece measures the same length as the back of the coat from the bottom to the underarm marker. Place a yarn marker as you did when working on the back of the coat at the side edge—the right-hand edge of the work—to indicate the start of the armhole.

Shaping the neck: Make sure you are beginning the first part of either afghan stitch pattern row. Work across the row in the pattern stitch to within 2 stitches of the end. Decrease 1 stitch at the left-hand, or neck, edge of the work (in the finished garment this will be the center front) in the following manner: skip the second-to-last stitch, remembering that for this pattern it will be a space, then work the last stitch. Continue to work in the pattern stitch, repeating the decrease at the neck edge on the first part of every row 24 (24, 25, 25, 26) more times. When you have 24 (26, 27, 29, 30) stitches remaining and the piece measures the same as the back of the coat to the shoulder, complete the second part of the pattern stitch row—if you have not already done so—ending at the right-hand, or side, edge of the work. Slip stitch across the entire row as you did when you were shaping the shoulders on the back of the coat, then fasten off.

The right front: Work this piece to correspond to the left-front section, reversing all the shaping. When you are decreasing below the point at which you place the underarm marker, the decreases will be made at the end of the row only (the left-hand side of the work).

When shaping the neck, again make sure you are beginning the first part of either afghan stitch pattern row. Then decrease at the beginning of the row (the right-hand edge of the work in this case) in the following manner: if you are working on row 2, skip the first two vertical bars; if you are working on row 3 skip the first three vertical bars; then continue to work in the pattern stitch across the remaining stitches.

THE SLEEVES

Using color A yarn, chain 49 (51, 53, 55, 57) stitches. Work even in the pattern stitch until the piece measures 17 1/2 inches, or the desired length, to the underarm. Work even for 2 inches more, then fasten off, without binding off. Repeat these directions to make the other sleeve.

THE FINISHING TOUCHES

Block each piece *(Glossary)*.

Sewing the seams: Following the instructions in the Appendix for weaving together knitted pieces, join the front sections to the back by weaving together the side seams, matching the markers at the underarms. Join the pieces at

each shoulder seam in the same manner. Weave together the underarm sleeve seams, then sew the sleeves in place. To make the garment completely reversible, weave the seam first with the dark-colored yarn, catching only the dark-colored stitches; then weave the seam again with the light-colored yarn, catching the light-colored stitches.

Be sure to carefully weave in any loose threads so that they are not visible on either side.

Making the belt: Using five strands of each of colors A and B together, make a chain that measures three times the size of your waist. Fasten off, then knot each end.

THE REVERSIBLE HAT

Using color A yarn, chain 55 stitches. Following the instructions for the two-color vertical bar stitch pattern *(page 154)*, work even on these stitches for approximately 7 inches, ending with a color A row. Now work 1 row of color A single crochet stitches, decreasing 1 stitch in each stitch across the row in the usual way *(Appendix)*. Fasten off.

Making the top: Weave the two short edges at each side of the work together as directed for weaving the seams of the reversible wrap coat *(above)*. Then thread three strands of color A yarn onto a large-eyed needle, such as a yarn or tapestry needle. Knot the strands at the end. Now draw the yarn through the row of single crochet stitches at the top of the work and pull the yarn tight to draw the work into a circle at the top. Secure the yarn tightly to the first stitch —where you began to draw the yarn through the single crochet stitches. Do not break off. Using the same yarn, weave together the remaining small open portion of the circle in the same manner as you did the side seams, thus forming the top of the hat.

Finishing the bottom edge: Using color A, work 1 row of single crochet stitches, decreasing 1 stitch in each stitch across the row as you did at the top of the work. Now using five strands each of colors A and B together, make a chain

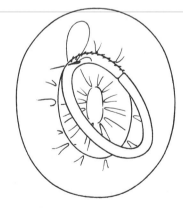

long enough to fit around your head comfortably. Fasten off. Join the first stitch to the last stitch you made to form a circle, then sew the two short ends together. Align one long edge of the chain to the row of single crochet stitches at the bottom of the hat; sew the chain in place, easing in any additional fullness as you go (drawing, left). Turn the work to the other side and attach the chain in the same way so the hat is completely reversible. Carefully weave in any loose threads so they do not show on either side.

THE REVERSIBLE SHOULDER BAG

Using color A yarn, chain 43 stitches. Following the instructions for the two-color vertical bar pattern (page 154), work even on these stitches for 24 inches. This piece will be folded in half lengthwise to form the body of the bag.

Connecting the side edges: Using five strands each of colors A and B together, make a chain 68 inches long. Fold the piece for the body of the bag in half, with the fold at the bottom, matching the two short ends at the top. Attach one end of the chain to one of the outside ends of the bottom fold. Then working from the bottom of the bag to the top opening, sew one side of the chain to the corresponding side edge of the bag. Next, attach the other side of the chain to the unattached portion of that side of the bag, thus forming the side seam. At this point, you will have used 12 inches of the 68-inch-long chain. Leave 44 inches of the chain free for the handle of the bag, then attach the re-

1

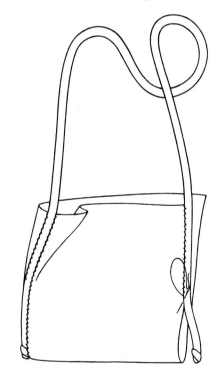

maining 12 inches of the chain to each of the other side sections as before, this time sewing from the top of the bag to the bottom fold (drawing 1).

Finishing the top edges: Make two more chains, each 11 inches long, in the same manner as you did the long chain for the sides and handle. Sew one long edge of one of these chains to the outside of the bag along one edge of the top opening (drawing 2). Attach the other chain to the other

2

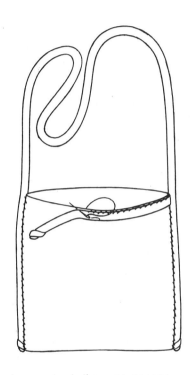

half of the top opening in the same manner.

Making the bag reversible: Now make two more 11-inch chains and two 12-inch ones. Turn the bag inside out. Sew each of the two 12-inch chains along the side edges of the bag directly opposite the chains forming the side seams on the reverse side. Attach the 11-inch chains to the edges of the top opening as you did on the other side of the bag.

Finishing the bag: Turn the bag to the reverse side once more. Position the bag so that the bottom edge is facing up. To reinforce the bottom, work 2 rows of single crochet stitches (Appendix) along the bottom edge (the original fold) in the following manner: using color A, attach the yarn at the right-hand edge of the bottom of the bag—as it is now positioned—at the point the side chain seam ends. Make the first row of single crochet, working each stitch under each of the top strands of the color B vertical bars along the bottom edge. Chain 1 and turn. Work the second row of single crochet in the usual manner, through the stitches of the previous row.

Carefully weave in any loose threads so that they are not visible on either side.

GLOSSARY

BACKSTITCH: To reinforce the beginning or end of a seam by making several machine stitches backward over the seam line.

BALLPOINT NEEDLE: A needle with a smooth rounded point that enables it to slip gently between the threads of such fabrics as knits and synthetics.

BAR TACK: The bar tack used for a corded buttonhole requires several zigzag stitches made very close together at the ends and perpendicular to the opening, and wide enough to span the cording without piercing it.

BASTE: To make long, loose stitches by hand or machine to hold pieces of fabric together temporarily. A line of basting is usually ended with a fastening or backstitch.

BATTING: A sheet of loosely matted fibers for use as insulation and interlining in garments, quilts and the like. Batting of various thicknesses is sold by the yard, in small packages and in bed sizes. Some batting comes already stitched between two layers of cloth, but most of it needs to be attached to fabric backing.

BIAS: A direction diagonal to that of the threads in woven fabric, i.e., the warp and woof, or "grains." A true bias is at a 45° angle to the grains.

BIAS TAPE: A folded strip of fabric cut on the bias, so that the strip will stretch smoothly to cover curved and straight edges.

BLOCK: To set the final shape of finished knitting or crocheting by pressing it with a warm iron through a damp cloth.

CURVED RULER: A special ruler used as a guide in drawing curves on patterns.

CUTTING LINE: A long, unbroken line marked on a pattern to indicate where it must be cut.

DART: A stitched fold, tapering to a point at one or both ends, to shape fabric around curves.

DRESSMAKER'S CARBON: Heavyweight white or colored carbon paper that is used with a tracing wheel to transfer pattern markings to fabric.

EASE: An even distribution of fullness in fabric, without perceptible gathers or tucks, that enables one section of a garment to be smoothly joined to another slightly smaller section.

FACING: A piece of fabric that is sewed along the raw edge of an opening, such as a neckline, and then turned to the inside to give the edge a smooth finish.

FUSIBLE WEB: A lightweight nonwoven material that forms a flexible, durable bond between layers of fabric. The bond is sealed by pressing the fabric with a dry or steam iron, depending on the product used.

GAUGE: The number of stitches and rows per inch in a piece of knitted or crocheted material.

GRADE: To trim each seam allowance within a multilayered seam to a different width to reduce bulk and make the seam lie flat.

GRAIN: In woven fabric, grain is the direction of the threads: the warp (the threads running from one cut end to the other) forms the lengthwise grain; the woof, or weft (the threads running across the lengthwise grain from one finished edge to the other), forms the crosswise grain.

GRAIN-LINE ARROW: The double-ended arrow marked on a pattern piece to indicate how the piece should be aligned with the fabric grains.

INTERFACING: A special firm fabric that is attached between two layers of garment fabric to stiffen, support or strengthen parts of the garment. A type of nonwoven interfacing can be fused to the fabric by ironing.

LINING: Fabric covering the inside of part or all of a garment.

NAP: On the surface of a fabric, the short fibers that are pulled and brushed in one direction.

PIVOT: A technique for machine stitching around angular corners by stopping the machine with the needle down at the apex of a corner, raising the presser foot, turning the fabric and then lowering the presser foot before continuing.

PRESHRINKING: The process of treating fabric to shrink it to an irreducible size before cutting. Washable fabric can be preshrunk simply by washing it as directed by the manufacturer.

PRESSER FOOT: The part of a sewing machine that holds down fabric while it is being stitched. A general-purpose foot has two prongs of equal length and is used for most stitching. A roller presser foot has two rollers with grids to prevent bulky or sheer fabric from sticking or slipping while being stitched. A straight-stitch foot has one long and one short prong and can be used for straight stitching and stitching fabrics of varying thicknesses. A two-pronged even-feed foot, used on machines that do zigzag stitching, has teeth on the bottom to move two or more layers of fuzzy, slippery or heavy fabric at the same speed. An overedge foot keeps narrow zigzag seams on knits from curling. A zipper foot has one prong and is used to stitch zippers and welting.

PRESSING CLOTH: A piece of fabric, preferably cotton drill cloth, that is placed between the iron and the garment when pressing.

RIB KNIT: A pattern of alternate knit and purl stitches which produces a very stretchy fabric.

SEAM ALLOWANCE: The extra fabric that extends outside a seam line.

SEAM LINE (also called stitching line): The long broken line marked on a pattern to indicate where a seam must be stitched.

SEAM TAPE: A flat tape of finishing fabric—rayon or nylon with a woven edge, or nylon or polyester stretch lace—usually 1/2 to 5/8 inch wide, sewed over a seam to reinforce it or used to finish hems.

STABILIZED SEAM: A seam that is reinforced with a strip of seam tape to add strength in an area of stress. Where a slight amount of flexibility is desired, in an area of moderate stress, the seam may be stabilized with bias tape.

STAY STITCHING: A line of machine stitching that is sewed along the seam line of a garment before the seam is finished to keep the edges from stretching.

TACK: Several stitches made in the same place to hold sections of a project or garment permanently in position.

TAILOR'S HAM: A firm, ham-shaped cushion with built-in curves that conform to various contours of the body. It is used for pressing areas that require shaping. One half of a ham is covered with cotton drill cloth for general pressing, the other half with soft wool—which is used when pressing woolen fabric to prevent shine.

THROAT PLATE: A flat metal piece, set into the base of a sewing machine, with a hole through which the needle passes as it stitches. A general-purpose throat plate has a wide hole that will accommodate any sideways motion of the needle. Many machines also have a second throat plate with a small hole to keep knits and soft fabrics from being pulled down into the machine and puckering during stitching. Most throat plates have guide lines marked on the right side to keep seams straight.

TOPSTITCHING: A line of ornamental machine stitching—usually parallel to a seam—on the visible side of a garment.

TRACING WHEEL: A small revolving disk attached to a handle and used with dressmaker's carbon to transfer pattern markings to fabric. Tracing wheels with smooth edges are used for knits to prevent snagging.

TWILL TAPE: A thin, extra-strong tape of twilled cotton or polyester used to reinforce seams.

ZIGZAG STITCHING: A serrated line of machine stitching.

HAND STITCHES

The diagrams below and on the following pages show how to make the elementary hand stitches and the knitting and crocheting stitches referred to in this volume.

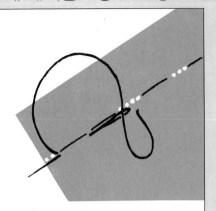

THE FASTENING STITCH
To end a row with a fastening stitch, insert the needle back 1/4 inch and bring it out at the point at which the thread last emerged. Make another stitch through these same points for extra firmness. To begin a row with a fastening stitch, leave a 4-inch loose end and make the initial stitch the same way as an ending stitch.

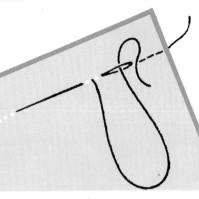

THE BACKSTITCH
Bring the needle up from the bottom layer of fabric and pull it through, leaving a 1-inch-long loose end. Insert the needle 1/8 inch to the right of where the thread emerged and bring it out 1/8 inch to the left of the thread. Continue inserting the needle 1/8 inch to the right, and bringing it out 1/8 inch to the left of the point where the thread last emerged. End with a fastening stitch on the bottom layer of fabric.

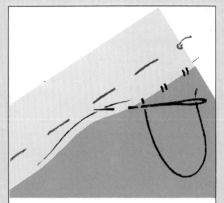

THE SLIP STITCH
Fold under the hem edge and anchor the first stitch with a knot inside the fold. Point the needle to the left. Pick up one or two threads of the garment fabric close to the hem edge, directly below the first stitch, and slide the needle horizontally through the folded edge of the hem 1/8 inch to the left of the previous stitch. Continue across in the same manner and end with a fastening stitch.

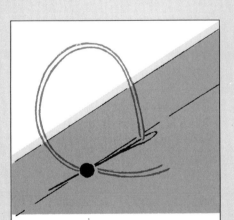

THE SINGLE TAILOR TACK
Using a double strand of unknotted thread, take a short stitch through the point to be marked, picking up the pattern piece and one or two layers of fabric, depending on whether or not the fabric is doubled. Leave 2-inch-long loose ends. Take another stitch through the same point, leaving a 2-inch loop on top of the pattern. End with at least 2 inches of loose thread.

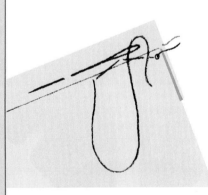

THE BLIND HEMMING STITCH
Baste the prepared hem to the garment 1/4 inch from the hem edge. Fold the hem along the basting so the hem lies beneath the garment and the unstitched edge projects above it. With knotted thread, insert the needle through one or two threads below the fold; pull the thread through. Pick up one or two threads above the fold and 1/2 inch to the left. Pull the thread through. Continue in this manner; end with a fastening stitch on the hem.

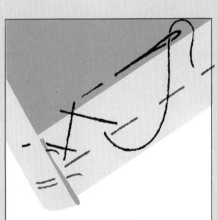

THE CATCH STITCH
Working from left to right, anchor the first stitch with a knot inside the hem 1/4 inch down from the edge. Pick up one or two threads of the garment directly above the hem; pull the thread through. Take a small stitch in the hem only (not in the garment), 1/4 inch down from the edge and 1/4 inch to the right of the previous stitch. End with a fastening stitch.

KNIT STITCHES

 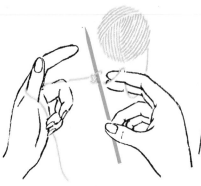 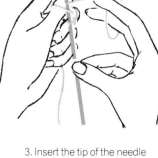 

CASTING ON STITCHES
1. Form a slipknot in the yarn, leaving a free end long enough for the number of stitches to be cast on (allow about 1 inch per stitch).

2. Slide a needle through the slipknot and hold the needle in your right hand. Loop the yarn attached to the ball over your right index finger and loop the free end of the yarn around your left thumb.

3. Insert the tip of the needle through the loop on your left thumb and bring the yarn attached to the ball under and over the needle from left to right.

4. Draw the tip of the needle back through the loop on your thumb, then slip the loop off your thumb. Pull the short end of the yarn down to tighten the loop, which is now a stitch. Repeat Steps 3 and 4 for the required number of stitches.

THE KNIT STITCH
1. Insert the right needle in the front of the stitch closest to the tip of the left needle, as shown. Bring the yarn under and over the right needle.

2. Pull the right needle back through the stitch, bringing with it the loop of yarn. Slide this loop—which is now a stitch—off the left needle and onto the right. Repeat Steps 1 and 2 for each knit stitch.

THE PURL STITCH
1. Insert the right needle into the stitch closest to the tip of the left needle, as shown. Bring the yarn around and under the right needle.

2. Push the needle back through the stitch, bringing with it the loop of yarn —which is now a stitch. Transfer this new stitch to the right needle, letting it slip off the left needle as you do so. Repeat Steps 1 and 2 for each purl stitch.

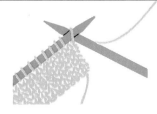   

INCREASING STITCHES
1. On a knit row, insert the right needle through the back of a stitch. Knit the stitch, but do not drop it off the left needle.

2. Knit the same stitch in the ordinary way, and transfer the two stitches to the right needle.

DECREASING STITCHES
1. Insert the right needle into two stitches instead of one, either from front to back as shown, for a knit stitch, or from back to front as for a purl stitch. Proceed as though you were knitting or purling one stitch at a time.

  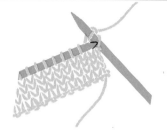

1. On a purl row, insert the right needle from right to left through the horizontal loop at the bottom of a stitch. Make a purl stitch but do not let it slide off the left needle.

2. Now insert the right needle into the vertical loop above the horizontal one. Purl the stitch in the ordinary way, and slide both loops onto the right needle.

BINDING OFF STITCHES
1. Knit (or purl) two stitches. Then insert the left needle through the front of the second stitch from the tip of the right needle.

2. With the left needle, lift the second stitch on the right needle over the first stitch and let it drop.

JOINING YARN

1. Wrap the new yarn around the working needle, leaving a long end. Use the new yarn to knit the next stitch. Break off the previous color if your instructions so indicate, leaving a long end.

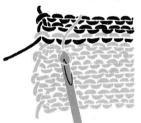

2. After knitting two or three rows with the new yarn, use a crochet hook to weave the loose ends of yarn through nearby stitches on the wrong side of the work.

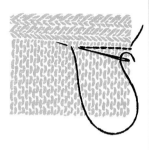

JOINING KNITTED PIECES

1. Knitted garments can be seamed by crocheting, weaving or sewing. For all three, place the edges together, wrong sides out, and align the stitches and rows. To crochet pieces together, insert a crochet hook through the first stitch on each edge, and draw a loop of new yarn through both stitches. Repeat on each pair of stitches, drawing the new loop through the loop on the hook.

2. To weave two pieces together, insert a blunt-tipped tapestry needle through the outermost stitch on each edge. Then turn the needle, and repeat. Continue weaving back and forth until the pieces are joined.

3. To sew two pieces together, insert a blunt-tipped tapestry needle through both pieces 1/4 inch below the aligned edges. Leaving a long end of yarn, insert the needle 1/4 inch to the right of the first stitch, and bring it out, from back to front, 1/4 inch to the left of the first stitch. Continue making stitches in this manner along the edges.

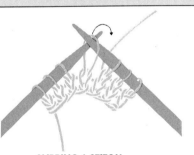

SLIPPING A STITCH

1. To slip a stitch as if to purl, insert the right needle into the next stitch as though you were going to purl, as shown, and transfer it from the left needle to the right without working it.

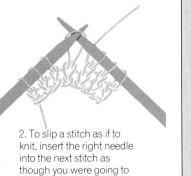

2. To slip a stitch as if to knit, insert the right needle into the next stitch as though you were going to knit, as shown, and transfer it from the left needle to the right without working it.

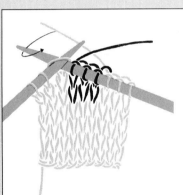

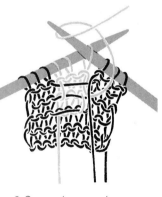

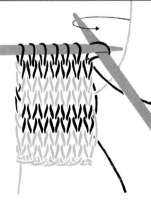

PICKING UP A DROPPED COLOR

1. On a knit row, reach under and behind the second color that you have been working to pick up the first color that you dropped earlier. Bring the strand of the first color forward and under the second color, and proceed to knit.

2. On a purl row, reach over and behind the first color and pick up the second color. Bring the strand under the first color and forward, and proceed to purl.

3. To carry a color from row to row, pick up the first color from where it was dropped on an earlier row in the same way you would in the middle of the row—from underneath, if you are beginning a knit row, as shown; or from over and behind if you are beginning a purl row.

THE CHAIN STITCH

1. Form a loose slipknot around the crochet hook, about 1 inch from the end of the yarn. Grasp the yarn attached to the ball with the tip of the hook and pull the yarn through the slipknot with the tip of the hook, as shown.

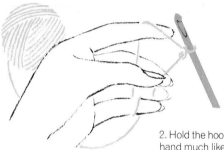

2. Hold the hook in your right hand much like a pencil. Place the yarn from the ball around the left little finger, then up and over the left index finger. Grasp the free end of the yarn between the thumb and middle finger of the left hand.

3. With your left index finger, bring the yarn from the back to the front of the hook and catch it under the tip of the hook.

4. Pull the tip of the hook through the loop in the hook, bringing the yarn with it to create the first chain stitch in the foundation chain. Repeat Steps 3 and 4 to form a chain of the desired length.

THE SINGLE CROCHET STITCH

1. To single crochet the first row after a foundation chain, insert the hook through the second chain stitch from the hook (arrow)—do not count the loop on the hook.

2. With two loops now on the hook, bring the yarn over the hook from back to front and catch it under the tip as shown. Then draw the yarn caught under the tip through the loop closest to the tip.

3. Bring the yarn over the hook again and draw it through both of the loops on the hook; there is now only a single loop on the hook. Insert the crochet hook into the next chain stitch and repeat Step 2. At the end of this and each successive row, chain one stitch if the next row will also be worked in single crochet stitches.

4. Turn the work to crochet back across the previous row. Insert the hook through both loops of the second stitch from the edge, as shown, and all subsequent stitches on this and all rows after the foundation chain.

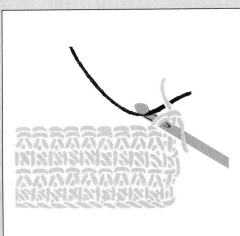

JOINING YARN

1. Join a new ball of yarn at the beginning of a row by drawing it through the first loop; leave a 1-inch-long end. Join a new color at the end of a row, working the last two loops on the hook with the new yarn.

2. When you have crocheted two or three rows, weave the loose ends of the yarn through nearby stitches with the crochet hook.

DECREASING STITCHES, SINGLE CROCHET

1. To decrease in a row of single crochet stitches, insert the hook into both loops of a stitch. Bring the yarn over the hook and draw it through the two loops closest to the tip; this leaves two loops on the hook.

2. Insert the hook through both loops of the next stitch. Bring the yarn over the hook and draw it through the two loops closest to the tip. Bring the yarn over the hook again and draw it through the three remaining loops on the hook.

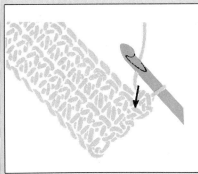

INCREASING STITCHES

Work one stitch, then insert the crochet hook back into the same stitch (arrow) and repeat the stitch.

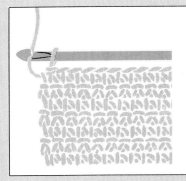

FASTENING OFF

Cut the yarn from the ball, leaving a 2-inch-long end. Pull this end through the loop on the hook to secure it and weave it through one or two nearby stitches.

BASIC SEWING TECHNIQUES

THE DUPLICATE PATTERN PIECE

1. To create a mirror-image pattern for any printed pattern piece that is designed to be cut in duplicate or on the fold of a fabric, first lay a sheet of tracing or other paper on a firm, flat surface. If necessary, tape sheets of paper together.

2. Pin the printed pattern piece, marked side up, to the paper.

3. Cut out the paper along the cutting lines of the printed pattern.

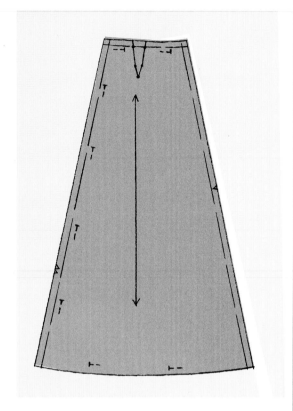

4. Without removing the pins, slide dressmaker's carbon, carbon side up, underneath the paper.

5. Use a tracing wheel to trace over all seam lines, notches and other markings on the printed pattern. Shift the position of the carbon as necessary.

6. Unpin the printed pattern piece, turn over the duplicate pattern and label it with the same number as the original.

7. If the printed pattern was designed to be laid out on the fold of the fabric, tape the duplicate pattern to the original along the fold line with both marked sides facing up.

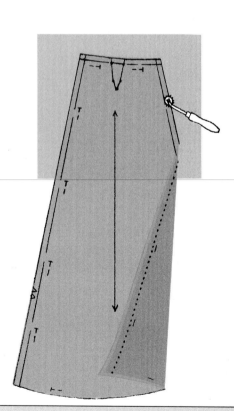

THE FLAT FELLED SEAM

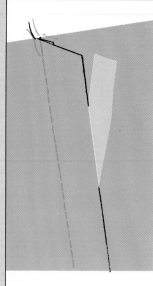

1. Make a plain seam with the wrong sides of the fabric facing out, and press both seam allowances in the desired direction.

2. Trim the top seam allowance to 1/2 inch and the underneath seam allowance to 1/8 inch.

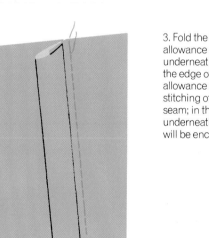

3. Fold the top seam allowance over the underneath one, lining up the edge of the top seam allowance along the stitching of the original plain seam; in this way the underneath seam allowance will be enclosed.

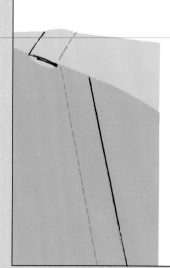

4. Turn the fold flat against the fabric to enclose the raw edge of the top seam allowance. Then pin or baste the fold in place.

5. Machine stitch along the folded edge. Remove the pins or basting and press.

CREDITS

Sources for illustrations and fashions in this book are shown below. Credits from left to right are separated by semicolons, from top to bottom by dashes.

ILLUSTRATIONS: Cover design courtesy of Carletex Corporation. 6,7—Michael Rinehart. 11—The Bettmann Archive; Sy Seidman; The Bettmann Archive; Sy Seidman; Culver Pictures, Inc. 12 through 19—Michael Rinehart. 20,21—Tomas Sennett. 24 through 29—Ryszard Horowitz. 34,35 —Drawings by John Sagan. 36 through 39 —Dan Budnik. 40,41—Tomas Sennett. 44,45—Richard Jeffery. 46—Ann Spanos Kuhn. 47 through 57—Drawings by John Sagan. 58—Ann Spanos Kuhn. 59 through 65—Drawings by John Sagan. 66—Ann Spanos Kuhn. 67 through 75—Drawings by Raymond Skibinski. 76—Ann Spanos Kuhn. 77,78,79—Drawings by John Sagan. 80—Ann Spanos Kuhn. 81 through 87 —Drawings by John Sagan. 88,89—Harald Sund. 92,93—Susan Woods. 94 through 101—Drawings by John Sagan. 102,103, 104—Susan Woods. 105 through 113 —Drawings by Raymond Skibinski. 114 —Susan Woods. 115 through 119—Drawings by Raymond Skibinski. 120,121— Susan Woods. 122 through 129—Drawings by John Sagan. 130,131—Susan Woods. 132 through 141—Drawings by Raymond Skibinski. 142,143—Tomas Sennett. 146, 147—Al Freni. 148—Drawing by Jean Held. 150,151—Al Freni. 152 through 155 —Drawings by Jean Held. 156 through 162 —Michael Rinehart. 164 through 168— Drawings by John Sagan. 169—Drawings by John Sagan (2)—Carolyn Mazzello (2). 170,171,172—Drawings by John Sagan.

FASHIONS: 6,7—Kasper for Joan Leslie. 12, 13—Outfits designed by Hanae Mori; Kasper for Joan Leslie; Mady Gerrard. All bags from Croutch & Fitzgerald Corp. 15 —Striped outfit from Right Bank Clothing Co., jewelry from Kenneth Lane Jewelry. 16,17—Beige slacks from Right Bank Clothing Co.; red outfit and hat designed by Mady Gerrard; reversible outfit designed by Ilie Wacs. All jewelry from Kenneth Lane Jewelry. 18,19—Gray and camel dress designed by Mady Gerrard, jewelry from Kenneth Lane Jewelry; outfit with print top and jewelry designed by Mary McFadden; aubergine outfit and jewelry designed by Mary McFadden. 24—Bag from Croutch & Fitzgerald Corp. Fabrics courtesy Claridge Knits, Inc.; Blue Ridge Winkler Textiles; Duplex International; Held Fabrics, Inc.; Held Fabrics, Inc.; Peter Pan Fabrics, Inc. 26,27 —Fabrics courtesy Carletex Corp.—Skinner Fabrics from The Singer Co.—Reeves Brothers, Inc.—American Silk Mills Corp. —Hale Fabrics Corp.—Carletex Corp. 28,29 —Suitcase from Saks Fifth Avenue, Inc. Fabrics courtesy Aberdeen Fabrics—Mittler of Switzerland—Far Eastern Fabrics —Filmax Textile Corp.—Far Eastern Fabrics —Far Eastern Fabrics. 44,45—Notions and supplies courtesy Belding Corticelli, Donahue Sales, The Pellon Corp., The Singer Company, J. P. Stevens Co., 3M Company, YKK Inc. 80—Outfit from Sportswork. 92,93—Striped fabric courtesy Far Eastern Fabrics, plain fabric courtesy Avila Fabrics. Coat made by Violet Mock. 102,103—Fabrics for outfit at left courtesy Carletex Corp., trim courtesy Knits Inc.; skirt fabric *(center)* courtesy Pressman Gutman Co.; body suit and scarf/halter fabric courtesy Stevecoknit Fabric Co.; pants fabric courtesy Duplex International. 104—Fabrics courtesy Carletex Corp. 114—Body suit and scarf fabric courtesy Stevecoknit Fabric Co., pants fabric courtesy Duplex International. 120,121 —Fabrics courtesy Held Fabrics Inc. 130-131—Bathing suit and djellaba made by Violet Mock. Shoes from Henri Bendel, Inc. 146,147—Knit swatches made by Annette Feldman. 150,151—Afghan crochet swatches made by Annette Feldman. 156,157—Knitted and crocheted garments made by Annette Feldman. 158—Knitted garments made by Annette Feldman. 162 —Afghan crocheted garments made by Annette Feldman.

ACKNOWLEDGMENTS

For their help in the preparation of this book the editors thank the following individuals: *in Danbury, Conn.:* Annette Partenio and James A. Severak, Branson Sonic Power Company; *in Elizabeth, New Jersey:* Sheral Rosen, The Singer Company; *in New York City:* Lewis Coco, J. P. Stevens & Co.; Virginia Haynes; Elisabeth Herriger, Vogue Magazine; Carol Horn; Calvin Klein; Judy Krull, Bloomingdale's; Catherine Lis, Saks Fifth Avenue; Daniel D. Powderly, Celanese Corp.; Belle Rivers, Donahue Sales; Betty Rollin; Cheryl Smith, Pellon Corporation; Frank Smith, Evan Picone; George Tay; Martha Taylor, YKK Zipper, Inc.; Myra Waldo.

The editors also thank *in New York City:* Abercrombie & Fitch Co.; Henri Bendel, Inc.; Butterick Fashion Marketing Company; The Celanese Corp. Fabric Library; Dan River, Inc.; Deering-Milliken Inc.; Delbon & Co.; E. I. Du Pont de Nemours & Co., Fashion Fabrics; Gloria Sachs Designs, Ltd.; Jacques Cohen, Ltd.; Knit-Away for Retail; Knits, Inc.; Miller Eye of New York; Rozette Knit Fabrics, Inc.; Saks Fifth Avenue; Texfi Industries; Vogue Fabric Library.

INDEX

Printed in U.S.A.